D1133231

THE TELEVISION SERIES

Lynda La Plante

Manchester University Press

THE
TELEVISION
SERIES

series editors

SARAH CARDWELL

JONATHAN BIGNELL

JULIA HALLAM

Lynda La Plante

LIBRARY ST. MARY'S COLLEGE

Manchester University Press

MANCHESTER AND NEW YORK

distributed exclusively in the USA by Palgrave

Published by Manchester University Press
Oxford Road, Manchester M13 9NR, UK
and Room 400, 175 Fifth Avenue, New York, NY 10010, USA
www.manchesteruniversitypress.co.uk

Distributed exclusively in the USA by
Palgrave, 175 Fifth Avenue, New York, NY 10010, USA

Distributed exclusively in Canada by
UBC Press, University of British Columbia, 2029 West Mall, Vancouver, BC, Canada V6T 1Z2

British Library Cataloguing-in-Publication Data
A catalogue record for this book is available from the British Library

Library of Congress Cataloging-in-Publication Data applied for

ISBN 0 7190 6548 8 *hardback*
EAN 978 0 7190 6548 4

First published 2005

14 13 12 11 10 09 08 07 06 05   10 9 8 7 6 5 4 3 2 1

Typeset in Scala with Meta display
by Koinonia, Manchester
Printed in Great Britain
by Bell & Bain Limited, Glasgow

Contents

List of illustrations

General editors' preface

Television is part of our everyday experience, and is one of the most significant aspects of our cultural lives today. Yet its practitioners and its artistic and cultural achievements remain relatively unacknowledged. The books in this series aim to remedy this by addressing the work of major television writers and creators. Each volume provides an authoritative and accessible guide to a particular practitioner's body of work, and assesses his or her contribution to television over the years. Many of the volumes draw on original sources, such as specially conducted interviews and archive material, and all of them list relevant bibliographic sources and further reading and viewing. The author of each book makes a case for the importance of the work considered therein, and the series includes books on neglected or overlooked practitioners alongside well-known ones.

In comparison with some related disciplines, Television Studies scholarship is still relatively young, and the series aims to contribute to establishing the subject as a vigorous and evolving field. This series provides resources for critical thinking about television. While maintaining a clear focus on the writers, on the creators and on the programmes themselves, the books in this series also take account of key critical concepts and theories in Television Studies. Each book is written from a particular critical or theoretical perspective, with reference to pertinent issues, and the approaches included in the series are varied and sometimes dissenting. Each author explicitly outlines the reasons for his or her particular focus, methodology or perspective. Readers are invited to think critically about the subject matter and approach covered in each book.

Although the series is addressed primarily to students and scholars of television, the books will also appeal to the many people who are interested in how television programmes have been commissioned, made and enjoyed. Since television has been so much a part of personal and public life in the twentieth and twenty-first centuries, we hope that the series will engage with, and sometimes challenge, a broad and diverse readership.

Sarah Cardwell
Jonathan Bignell

Acknowledgements

Thanks to the BFI Library staff and the British Universities Film and Video Council for helping with research and locating copies of La Plante's works, to Mathew Frost and Kate Fox at Manchester University Press for their patience and support, to the series editors Jonathan Bignell and Sarah Cardwell for their helpful comments on the text and to Nickianne Moody and her students at Liverpool John Moores University for comments on an earlier draft.

On a more personal note, this book is dedicated to Jude Lobely and Penny French for their strength and fortitude; love and thanks to you both.

Introduction

Award-winning writer Lynda La Plante is one of Britain's most visible and successful screenwriters. During the course of a prolific career her crime thrillers have persistently explored controversial issues of violence, paedophilia and pornography, often focusing on the role of the police and the legal profession and the psychology of criminals. It is within this popular genre, beginning with *Widows* in 1983 and continuing with *Prime Suspect* in 1991, that she has been most innovative and found her greatest success. By the end of the 1990s, La Plante was dubbed by some critics 'the queen of crime' and it is this aspect of her work that forms the principal axis of this account of her writing for television. As one of the most commercially successful writers in Britain and as a woman who has made award-winning interventions in a TV genre formerly considered a bastion of masculine values, her work invites an exploration of the relationship between commercial authorship and critical contexts, with issues of gender, representation, formal experimentation and authorial celebrity well to the fore. A tripartite focus on three of her key works first investigates their innovative and ground-breaking aspects through an examination of the relationship between content, context and formal structures. Second, it seeks to place La Plante's generic interventions within the broader context of changes in the broadcasting industry, with a particular focus on the implications of those changes for women in terms of creating and making television drama, as well as considering aspects of female representation on the screen. Third, attention is paid to questions of critical value and judgement; in spite of winning numerous awards, La Plante's thrillers are often condemned for their violent and graphic content and their melodramatic style. These aesthetic issues are traced against the background of changes in the industry and La Plante's decision to start her own production company in order to retain creative and financial control of her work.

If there is a consistent theme throughout La Plante's work, it is the attempt to deal with male violence by, as she puts it, 'getting inside it', examining its manifestations and the psychological makeup and motivations of those who perpetrate it. Her work often depicts the disturbing consequences of male violence through graphically explicit images of mutilated and dead female bodies which some critics find exploitative, sensationalist and manipulative. In contrast to these darker aspects of her work, drama commissioners and critics alike expect La Plante to create strong female characters who nonetheless retain their femininity, characters who represent the diversity of modern British women, crusading characters who appeal to feminist and non-feminists alike, men as well as women. Often held up as a representative of what a woman working in the creative side of the television industry can achieve, La Plante is expected to be more alert to issues of moral and political correctness than her male peer group. This is a tall order for a popular writer, and unsurprisingly La Plante has little interest in trying to fulfil it. She rejects, for example, any explicit alignment with feminist politics or any other political ideologies, although in practice she has strong sympathies with issues of sexual discrimination in the workplace and presents herself in interviews as something of a female pioneer, as indeed she is. Her first thriller, *Widows*, was the first crime serial to be written and produced by a female team and for this reason alone is a milestone in UK television drama. Focusing on the stories of the bereaved wives of a criminal gang rather than the men themselves or the police investigating their crimes, *Widows* broke the conventions of the 1970s crime series and ushered in a new era of female-centred drama. A second series of *Widows* followed in 1985; then, owing at least in part to rapid changes in the UK television industry, five years elapsed before La Plante had another drama accepted for television.

Prime Suspect, commissioned by Granada for the ITV network in 1990, is undoubtedly La Plante's most successful and well-known series, winning numerous awards at home and in the US as well reaching an international audience and making stars of its author and leading actor. The series is built around the career of a senior female detective in the Metropolitan police force, Detective Chief Inspector Jane Tennison, memorably performed by Helen Mirren, who ruthlessly plays the boys' game in order to achieve her ambitions. In the form of a number of two-part four-hour mini-series, the series charts Tennison's career trajectory against a plethora of misogynistic working practices in the police force and her personal failure to sustain a long-term relationship.

Following the critical and commercial success of the third series of *Prime Suspect*, La Plante formed her own production company to produce and manage her work. In one of the first series produced by her new company, *Trial and Retribution* (1996), La Plante offers viewers a different perspective on the crime series, taking them through the processes and procedures of detective work as police hunt for a missing child who is eventually found sexually abused and murdered. The series places the economic dictates and politics of police work under the microscope, examining the work of the crime prosecution service and the lawyers that run the system as well as the psychological effects of the murder on the bereaved family and the young policeman who finds the body. Unlike TV crime series that seek to reassure viewers that public institutions are effective and trustworthy, *Trial and Retribution* offers an uncomfortable viewing position by presenting conflicting accounts of events from witnesses and relatives of the murdered child.

As well as discussing La Plante's key innovations in some depth and elaborating on her contributions to the crime series, a second axis of this account highlights the growing role and significance of La Plante as a producer of her own work. One of the first women writers to break through the glass ceiling in an industry where, historically, women have been disadvantaged by virtue of their gender, not their creative ability, La Plante has fought to achieve the critical recognition that she is so obviously entitled to. Furthermore, by storming a culturally prestigious area of television production traditionally reserved for men, she challenges essentialist critical positions that identify women as writers (and viewers) primarily of soap and melodrama. Because she is best known for dramas that feature strong, purposeful women determined to find their own way in areas of life often considered the principal domain of men, many women, including women in the television industry, regard La Plante as something of a feminist pioneer in spite of her attempts to avoid the label. In interviews she avoids the issue, denying that she writes for any overt political purposes and prevents herself being branded a political writer by the simple technique of evasion. Andrew Billen, for example, found it difficult to draw from her any acknowledgement of political inference in her work because she steadfastly maintains that everything she writes is true, based on fact, the result of her personal research. When asked about her writing style and her technique La Plante presents herself as more akin to an investigative journalist than an imaginative storyteller, someone who roots out unsavoury facts that often remain hidden and need to be confronted. She stresses the research aspect of her projects, talks about the people she has interviewed and the problems of depicting authentic accounts of their experiences. For Billen, the problem is not so much that he doubts her word as that her writing does not always convince

(Billen 1996: 6). It is perhaps because definitions of quality in British television continue to rest on humanist foundations which favour judgements of realism and authenticity of character (concepts that La Plante herself mobilises in defence of her work) that, in spite of La Plante's success in an industry and a genre where women writers have failed to make an impact in the past, critics have often failed to engage with the more innovative aspects of her work. These issues are discussed in more depth in Chapter 4.

By the mid-1990s La Plante had achieved unprecedented creative control and jurisdiction of her projects, a situation that enabled her to experiment with innovative risk-taking formats and subject matter as well as producing ruthlessly commercial dramas and novels. The growth in the number of channels available in the UK from only three in 1980 (BBC 1, BBC 2 and ITV) to the proliferation of terrestrial, cable and satellite channels available today has transformed the ways in which television is produced, distributed and viewed. An increased choice of entertainment options and the changing function of what once was thought of as 'the box in the corner' means that television is now less a focus of family life, more an individual lifestyle appendage. Multi-occupied homes have multiple sets, with channels and programmes targeted to appeal to particular groups. With competition to attract well-heeled consumers and deliver them as audiences to advertisers steadily increasing throughout the industry, UK terrestrial broadcasting has shifted in ethos from the public-service principles that underpinned its governance in the 'duopoly' era (1956-82) to the 'lighter touch' free-market principles that inevitably permeate multi-channel broadcast environments (see, for example, Crisell 1997; Smith 1998). Within this context, drama series and serials made to appeal to commercially targeted groups continue to attract large numbers of viewers and are significant ratings winners for their channels, both terrestrial and satellite (Paterson 1999; Buonanno 2000).

La Plante's writing career spans the twenty years in which these changes have taken place; she has created more than twenty dramas for UK television, five mini-series for US television and has written seven novels (a list of La Plante's works is given in the Appendix). As British broadcasting rapidly grew more like its transatlantic neighbour in structure as well as content during the 1990s, La Plante sought to retain creative control of her work by adopting the North American writer/producer model. Since 1997, La Plante has turned away from her more experimental work to develop strongly commercial and arguably 'trans-atlantic' productions such as *Supply and Demand* (1996, 1997), *Killer Net* (1997) and *Mind Games* (2000) while at the same time nurturing

the American market for her work. More recent dramas for UK television continue to tread what has become familiar and successful
territory: *The Commander* (ITV 2003) stars Amanda Burton as a senior
police officer in the Metropolitan Police and a new series of *Trial and
Retribution* continues to be broadcast annually on ITV terrestrial at the
time of writing this account in 2004.

Since taking control of her own scripts and ideas in 1994, when she
started her own production company, La Plante has increasingly looked
to the lucrative North American TV drama and film market, joining
forces in 2001 with Sophie Balhetchett to start a new company to make
feature films. Like La Plante's first co-producer, Verity Lambert,
Balhetchett has a distinguished record as a producer: in 1989 she was
responsible for *The Manageress*, a drama series featuring a woman as
the new manager of a struggling football club; in 1992 she produced a
four-part adaptation of Mary Wesley's novel *The Camomile Lawn* (both
Zed Ltd Productions for Channel 4); as part of Tony Garnet's renowned
company World Productions she produced dramas such as *Ballykissangel*
and *Ultraviolet*. La Plante and Balhetchett's new company, Cougar
Films, had a number of feature-film projects in the pipeline at the time
this book went to press.

The brief biography that opens the first chapter is drawn from
numerous interviews with journalists printed between 1984 when the
success of *Widows* first alerted the press to her work and 2001 when she
received the Dennis Potter award for writing from the British Academy
of Film and Television Arts (BAFTA). It is a compilation of the public
knowledge she has chosen to reveal about herself rather than an in-
depth search through her personal archives. A request that she assist
this project by providing access to press cuttings and interviews was
rejected in October 2002 due to the pressure of other commitments;
she is not prepared, as yet, to open these to academic scrutiny. La Plante
suffers from dyslexia, a condition unrecognised in her childhood. This,
combined with a lack of higher education, has made her wary of the
critical establishment. She pursues popular rather than critical success,
placing far more faith in her viewers and professional colleagues than in
critical opinion. Nonetheless, given that all biographical writing is a
form of storytelling, an account of La Plante's life based on anecdotes
recounted to journalists (usually with the intention of promoting her
latest work) is no less an account than one based on personal memory,
reflection and recollection. In fact it seems a highly appropriate way to
begin discussing the work of an author who admits unashamedly that
her prime motivation for writing is to make money and to be successful.
La Plante's fundamental talent is to tell stories that entertain; if, as part

of that process, she reveals hidden prejudices in our social institutions and questions some of our attitudes and assumptions it is because she is part of the more general mood for change that transformed UK society in the last twenty-five years of the twentieth century. In this sense, there are obvious parallels with her literary 'sisters' writing crime novels, particularly those of a liberal and neo-liberal disposition such as Ruth Rendell in the UK and Sara Paretsky and Patricia Cornwell in the US. These themes will be taken up in more depth in the analysis of key works in the chapters that follow.

Women and television

By the year 2001 the battle to establish women dramatists in the television industry had ostensibly been won; not only had La Plante received the Dennis Potter writer's award but there was increasing acknowledgement that some of the most interesting and critically acclaimed drama on television was being written by women.[1] As well as writing drama, a number of women had started their own companies specialising in the production of drama. Verity Lambert, former head of drama at Thames Television, was one of the first women to establish herself as an independent producer with her company Cinema Verity in 1985. La Plante followed suit in 1995. By the end of the decade, a number of companies run by women were producing critically acclaimed drama. Red Productions, for example, was run by former script editor Nicola Schindler (*Queer as Folk* (C4 1998), *Cutting It* (BBC 2003–4) and *Linda Green* (2001–2)), and Shed was created by the former managing director of London Weekend Television Eileen Gallagher with ex-Granada staffwriters Brian Park, Maureen Chadwick and Ann McManus (*Bad Girls* (ITV 1998–), *Footballers' Wives* (ITV 2003–)). Roll'em Productions (UK) is writer Kay Mellor's company, responsible for dramas such as *Fat Friends* (ITV 2000, 2003) and *Between the Sheets* (ITV 2003).

In the early 1980s the picture was very different; there were no independent UK production companies making programmes for British TV channels. Most drama was produced in-house by the BBC and the 'big five' network companies who held ITV franchises or was imported from abroad, usually from American or Australian production companies and distributors. Very few women were employed as writers, producers, directors or technicians and there were very few roles for leading female characters in prime-time series and serials. Women in production worked primarily as secretaries and production assistants (jobs traditionally regarded as female) and in drama they were cast as wives, girlfriends and mothers or, if they worked, as cleaners, nurses, secretaries and sex workers; images of successful career women were few and far between. Arguably, the most commonly featured working women were prostitutes, a role Lynda La Plante often played in ITV dramas during the 1970s under her stage name of Lynda Marchal.

The first part of this chapter provides a brief biographical sketch of La Plante's career, mapping her progression from her early days as a drama student at the Royal Academy of Dramatic Art (RADA) in London to her appearances in crime dramas such as *The Sweeney* (1975–8), made by Euston Films Ltd for Thames Television. It was here she met Verity Lambert, who would later produce her first television drama *Widows*. The significance of Lambert's encouragement at this early stage in La Plante's career as a writer cannot be underestimated; Lambert was one of the very few women in a position of power and responsibility in television at that time. *Widows* was the first crime thriller written and produced by women to occupy the male-dominated mid-evening screen space of prime-time drama. The series competed head to head with the BBC's imported US ratings booster *Dallas* in the popular 9–10 p.m. slot when viewing was at its peak; *Widows* won a decisive victory, attracting eleven million viewers.

La Plante's new writing career had taken off in style. Numerous mini-series, series, serials, novels and screenplays have followed since, with *Prime Suspect* achieving international success and critical recognition. In spite of this success in a male-dominated industry where women have had to struggle to be noticed, her work has suffered critical neglect; the award-winning *Prime Suspect* was regarded by some critics (including feminist critics) as little more than an opportunity to enhance ratings, as broadcasters hungry for new audiences embraced the equal-opportunities agenda (Brunsdon 1998). Such a view takes no account of La Plante's involvement in the struggles of women working in television to achieve not only equality of representation *on* the screen but equality of participation in the creative and production process *behind* the screen. The second part of this chapter maps the broad contours of this struggle, placing La Plante's career trajectory in the context of the mood for change and decisive action that shaped gender relations in the television industry between 1975 when La Plante was still playing prostitutes and good-time girls and the early 1990s when, with the international success of *Prime Suspect*, it looked as if the barriers to female success in the industry were finally breached and torn down.

A brief biographical sketch

La Plante, born Lynda Titchmarsh in 1943, grew up on Merseyside the middle child in a family of five with an older brother and a younger sister. Her father was a salesman, her mother a housewife; improving family fortunes saw the family move from their small terraced house to a larger, more salubrious residence by the time Lynda was twelve. When she talks about her childhood, La Plante recalls the wildness of the seashore and the surrounding countryside, Wellington boots and bicycle rides, the smells of strawberries, blackberries and wildflowers, memories for the most part swept away by redevelopment, modernisation and the onward march of the suburbs into the surrounding woods and fields. In those days, Crosby was a seafaring town with close links to the docks. Some of Lynda's uncles were dockers and sailors; one was a sailing-ship expert who travelled the world by sea. La Plante describes him as 'tattooed from head to toe' and able to speak twelve languages.

> He had a ponytail and a navy pinstriped suit with a white T-shirt. I'd never seen anybody wear that. He would produce a long blade knife and say it was for committing hari-kari. His house smelled of tobacco and incense and he had lions on the wall. He was a raconteur and a warrior. I was so receptive to him. He always used to say 'Be a warrior in life, don't be a wimp'. (Wueratna 1996: 42)

La Plante has never been much of a wimp or a shrinking violet; by her own admission as a child she was bossy and an exhibitionist, often putting on shows for the family where she would sing, dance and tell stories. In interviews, she has talked about her early fascination with storytelling, honing her skills on her younger sister whom she enjoyed terrifying with horrific tales of the unexpected late at night. There is a sadder side to these outward shows of childish exhibitionism and exuberance, though: her older sister died tragically in a road accident aged only five while her mother was pregnant with Lynda; she grew up distracting her parents from the void left in family life by playing the household star (Weale 2000: 16). In spite of this sadness, La Plante has always resisted the kind of simplistic psychological analysis of her work that associates childhood and early life with the themes of her stories. She remembers her childhood as a happy time; asked by Mark Lawson in an interview for the *Guardian* if her parents' sorrow impinged upon her in any way, she replied that rather than becoming overprotective of their offspring, her parents withdrew from them to protect themselves from ever being hurt by the loss of a child in quite the same way again. As a result, the children were more or less free to do as they pleased. Only on one occasion, when questioned by a BBC religious programmes presenter, has La Plante talked about sometimes feeling the spiritual presence of her dead sister around her. She denies any autobiographical relationship between the themes of her dramas and her early life but accepts that if there is a connection it may have something to do with the distance between these idyllic memories and the very different worlds she depicts in her stories (Lawson 1998: 86–7).

La Plante attended a local private girls' school; her mother, concerned that she might develop a Liverpool accent, sent her to elocution lessons. She claims her desire to become an actress stemmed from falling in love with her elocution teacher and wanting to talk and be like her. At sixteen she won a scholarship to study for a Diploma in Dramatic Arts at the Royal Academy of Dramatic Art and left Merseyside for London. Initially, she hated it; one of her earliest lessons was with a voice tutor who wanted to prove how limiting regional accents were (Wueratna 1996: 42). Received pronunciation and standard English were the rule in drama college in those days; class status mattered even more than money in Britain's elite cultural institutions in spite of the fashion for northern working-class realism in plays and novels such as John Osborne's *Room at the Top* and Alan Sillitoe's *Saturday Night and Sunday Morning*. Surprisingly, La Plante makes no mention of the influence of British realism and the 'New Wave' on her subsequent style as a novelist and scriptwriter, perhaps because, like many young people of the day, her cultural horizons looked out to Europe and the work of French New Wave filmmakers such as François Truffaut; she cites *Jules et Jim* (Truffaut 1962) as one of her favourite films (Lawson 1998: 86–7).

On leaving RADA, La Plante auditioned for Laurence Olivier at the National Theatre; it was his amusement with the name Titchmarsh that convinced her to adopt the stage name Lynda Marchal. For the next twenty years of her life, La Plante pursued a successful career as a stage and television actress, treading the boards of provincial theatres such as the Liverpool Playhouse with actors who later became household names, including Anthony Hopkins. An acclaimed appearance in a Whitehall farce with the popular comic actor Brian Rix in 1972 led to appearances at the National Theatre with the Royal Shakespeare Company. She regards playing the leading role in a production of *Calamity Jane* at the Sheffield Crucible Theatre in 1974 as the pinnacle of her stage career (Moir 1992: 19). Supporting roles in peak-time TV dramas followed, including *The Professionals* (ITV 1977–83), *The Gentle Touch* (ITV 1980–4) and *Bergerac* (BBC 1981–91); she also played minor characters in Euston Films productions made for the ITV network, such as *The Sweeney* (ITV 1975–8). It was here, while playing a prostitute, that she met Verity Lambert, then head of drama at Thames, and script editor

Linda Agran and felt able to express her dissatisfaction with the restricted diet of secondary roles available to women actors. Tired of playing second fiddle to leading male characters as their girlfriends, wives and prostitutes, La Plante was encouraged by Lambert and Agran to write a crime series with women at the centre of the action.

During her acting years, La Plante occasionally experimented with writing, beginning with several plays, four of which were produced (one at the Belgrade Theatre, Coventry); all were critically slaughtered. A credit as a member of the writing team on ATV's *The Kids From 47a*, broadcast between 1973 and 1976, points to an early ambition to write for television; she was in her late thirties by the time she finally achieved her goal. In interviews she steadfastly maintains that she started writing television drama because of sloppy scripts and a paucity of good roles for women. The following anecdote has become part of popular La Plante mythology. It was while playing a prostitute in an episode of ITV's *The Gentle Touch* (1980–4), the first television drama to feature a female detective inspector (played by Jill Gascoine), that she submitted four ideas for storylines to the producers. Ironically, considering her later success with *Prime Suspect*, none of the outlines focused on Gascoine's character and all were rejected, but on one of them, a story about the wives of a gang of robbers carrying out a robbery on their own, someone had written, 'This is brilliant' (Royal Television Society 1993: 10). This gave her sufficient motivation to develop the plot into a series initially called 'The Women' which later, under the guidance of Verity Lambert and Linda Agran at Euston Films, became the serial known today as *Widows*.

In 1982, inspired by the Falklands War, she began to map out ideas for *Civvies*, a six-part drama focused on the lives of a group of men who had recently left the army. Although *Widows* was highly successful and critically acclaimed, the follow up, *Widows II*, was less well received; La Plante disowned it initially after differences of opinion over casting and direction. Subsequent projects failed to ignite the enthusiasm of TV producers; *Civvies* remained on the BBC shelf for a further four years until the success of *Prime Suspect* proved again her ability to attract the television audience (Stoddart 1992: 6). In the meantime La Plante turned her attention to writing novels, completing three before she secured her next drama commission: *The Legacy* (1987), *The Talisman* (1989) and *Bella Mafia* (1991), all of which sold in respectable numbers.

Her fortunes turned again at the end of the 1980s when she attended a meeting with programme executives at Granada Television. La Plante was asked if she had a police series in mind; she claims she had not, but on the spot came up with the idea of a woman detective who takes over the running of a murder squad. Capturing the imagination of the executives through her ability to tell the story by acting out the parts, she presented them with an off-the-cuff title, *Prime Suspect*. Some weeks later, armed with a commission and fired with enthusiasm, she rang Scotland Yard and asked to talk to a senior female detective. The list of potential candidates was a small one; only four women at that time held senior positions in the Metropolitan Police, one of whom, Jackie Malton, agreed to be interviewed. Malton became the role model on whom La Plante based DCI Jane Tennison, the character that Helen Mirren turned into a 1990s icon of the professional career woman. The huge success both commercially and critically of the first *Prime Suspect* led to two sequels in 1992 and 1993, *Prime Suspect 2* and *Prime Suspect 3*, securing Mirren's position at the apex of British television acting and confirming La Plante as a creator of innovative and popular television drama.

As the awards mounted for the first *Prime Suspect*, La Plante was busy developing the projects that she had been unable to persuade anyone to produce following the second series of *Widows*. Again, it was a female producer, this time Ruth Caleb at the BBC, who gave the green light to her next series, *Civvies* (BBC 1992), a six-part drama based on the post-army lives of a group of paratroopers who had seen active service in Northern Ireland and the Falklands War. The male characters at the heart of the drama are severely traumatised by the effects of violence and suffer from what was a widely debated and contentious psychological condition at the time, post-traumatic shock. *Civvies* created a storm of controversy, condemned by the military and *Daily Telegraph* readers alike primarily because of its seemingly authentic depictions of violence. In spite of its mixed reception, *Civvies* confirmed La Plante's ability to write searing, uncompromising realist dramas.

In an interview with Lesley White for the *Sunday Times Magazine* in 1995, La Plante talks about her working methods, claiming that all her characters are based on people she has met (White 1995: 38, 41). By this time she was working on *The Governor*, a series idea that developed during the course of her research for *Civvies*, which had involved visiting prisons and talking to prisoners. White contends that while other writers talk about their inspiration, La Plante, 'like a scientist in a lab', only talks about her research. Every character, every line of dialogue is based on someone she has met, something she has heard. 'It is the ordering that is the art. Someone can tell you a story and it can bore the pants off you. I inject something personal, twist it' (White 1995: 41). La Plante has based her reputation as a writer on the thoroughness of her research, the accuracy of even the smallest of details and the authenticity of her stories, a technique she has consciously perfected. She claims, for example, that she met the four men who form the basis of the characters in *Civvies*, took them under her wing and employed them as caterers. Her husband guaranteed the bank loan for the mini-cab company they wanted to start but the plan backfired and by the time the BBC bought the series, every one of the ex-paratroopers was in prison for crimes that ranged from armed robbery to murder. She began visiting the men in prison and realised that they were all psychologically disturbed; 'they weren't sleeping, they were having sweats, they were suffering from post-traumatic stress' (White 1995: 41). Her prison visits continued as she worked as a writer in residence and ran drama workshops at various institutions around the country. It was during the course of this work that she met Alison Gomme, governor of Erlestoke Prison near Devizes, who at the age of thirty-three was the youngest prison governor in England and one of the few women running a men's prison. Gomme does not deny that she helped La Plante with the research for *The Governor*, first aired on ITV in 1995 with Janet McTeer in the leading role.

In the three years between *Civvies* (1992) and *The Governor* (1995), eight other dramas written by La Plante or developed from her original storylines were broadcast on UK terrestrial, including *Prime Suspect 2* (1993) and *Prime Suspect 3* (1993), *Seconds Out* (Granada Television for the BBC 1992), *Framed* (Anglia 1992), *Seekers* (Central 1993), *Comics* (Cinema Verity for Channel 4 1993), *The Lifeboat* (Bloom Street Productions for the BBC 1994), and *She's Out* (a La Plante Production and Cinema Verity Production for Carlton Television 1995). The success of *Prime Suspect* enabled La Plante and her husband Richard, a North American rock singer whom she married in the mid-1970s, to move into a mansion in Surrey and buy a second home on Long Island. Like La Plante, Richard was also an aspiring writer, but although he published several novels success evaded him; as Lynda's career reached new heights of success with her high-profile screenplays catapulting her novels on to the bestseller lists, their relationship faltered and failed. Stories of the marital breakdown appeared in the popular press, with La Plante talking publicly for the first time about her inability to have children and the various treatments she had taken for infertility.

In spite of her personal problems, on the business front La Plante's star continued to rise; she had become Britain's most popular and prolific television dramatist. She decided to use her success and reputation to take creative and financial control of her work and start her own production company, turning her attention to the American market. She claims that the desire to control her own productions was fuelled when she was informed by Granada Television that the American Emmy award for *Prime Suspect* belonged not to her but to the producer.

'I thought of all the time I'd spent in Aids clinics, all that time with the police, to get that story and then the producer hired a crew and filmed it! I didn't own it. I was just for hire' (Lawson 1998: 86). La Plante left *Prime Suspect* with Granada and turned her attention to new projects. *The Governor* (directly commissioned for the ITV network) was the first series to be written and produced by Lynda La Plante herself and marks the turning point in her career.

Verity Lambert, her former producer and mentor at Thames, was not surprised by her declaration of independence: 'There are two kinds of writer. Those who have no interest in how it all gets put on and those who fret about every detail. Even as a novice writer, Lynda knew what she wanted' (Lawson 1998: 86). By this time Lambert was running her own production company; she had taught La Plante not only about the minutiae of drama production such as pace and timing, essential to the success of popular series and serials, but also about the business side of the industry. A personal friend as well as a professional associate, La Plante is a great admirer of Lambert and aware of how Lambert's preparedness to give new writers a chance helped forge her own career. In her view Lambert 'has probably done more for the television industry than any other single female producer' (Jones 1994: 7). Such accolades to other women in the industry do not fall lightly from La Plante's tongue. Commenting in an interview with Andrew Billen on a controversial speech she gave at the annual award ceremony of Women in Film and Television in 1995, she stated: 'Just as other women have made my career, there have been women who have been very, very destructive ... the only time the knives have been out for me have been from other women' (Billen 1996: 6).

A second series of *The Governor* followed in 1996, along with a two-hour screenplay, *Supply and Demand*, and what was to be the first of an ongoing 2 × 2-hour mini-series, *Trial and Retribution*. The critical response to all these dramas was muted; even *Trial and Retribution*'s revolutionary split-screen format failed to ignite much excitement, perhaps because by this time the popular melodramatic format of *The Governor* was seen as more typical of La Plante's output. For critics working within a framework of evaluation dominated by questions of realism as the measure of quality drama, *The Governor* was far too sensational. Journalistic response to *Trial and Retribution*'s non-traditional format was cast in a similar vein, claiming that the tripartite screen would only serve to confuse viewers, who would find it difficult to read three images at once on their small domestic TV screens. La Plante responded by arguing that such comments underestimated the abilities of viewers accustomed to watching complex advertising campaigns and TV news bulletins, both of which were often more complex than her split-screen narration (Power 1997: 20).

La Plante's conviction about the ways in which the television image was changing to meet the challenge of the multi-channel viewing environment now seems prescient, her treatment of the narration in *Trial and Retribution* moving British television drama one step closer to the sought-after holy grail of interactive narrative involvement. Challenging fixed viewpoints of detection and resolution, La Plante pulled traditional anchors of pleasure and reassurance in the crime series from under viewers' feet, creating unease and anxiety not only about the guilt (or not) of the prime suspect but about the processes of the legal system and the machinations of justice itself.

Trial and Retribution was followed in 1997 by *Killer Net*, a series with a more traditional format but this time a prescient theme: Internet pornography and paedophilia. Following the highly publicised spate of police raids on Internet paedophile rings in the US and UK in 2002, such a theme no longer seems far fetched or controversial, but in 1997 the Internet was still regarded primarily as a force for good in society that would enable every household easy access to the benefits of education and information, on-line shopping and e-mail. The more disturbing possibilities inherent in a new medium operating in virtual space without censorship or censure had barely been acknowledged. La Plante's research for the series revealed what has since become common knowledge: that a large percentage of Internet traffic is devoted to pornography and paedophilia. At the time, however, her ideas seemed exaggerated to many critics, perhaps in part because her public image and celebrity persona works against constructing her as someone to be taken seriously, a writer with 'big' ideas. Josephine Monroe, for example, in an interview arranged to promote her latest drama, describes her as 'complete with fake American accent, draped in animal prints and holding court in her west end offices', looking 'more like an airport novelist than a serious dramatist' (Monroe 1998: 16). For critics such as Monroe those aspects of her dramas that have mass appeal are often the most annoying, debasing what they regard as the more interesting aspects of authentic depiction of character and plot. The tension between melodrama, spectacle and a realist claim to authenticity that lies at the heart of La Plante's work is often critically evaluated as problematic, implying that entertainment and art cannot, by their very nature, be part of the same text, be produced by the same person or belong to the same (authorial) space. These ideas will be opened up and explored in the chapters that follow.

Struggles for equality

It's obvious – especially to women who work in the industry – that
there'll never be real equality on the screen until there's equality behind
the camera. (Koerber 1977: 141–2)

La Plante's career as a writer is closely tied to the struggles for female
equality in broadcasting; as an actress, she was highly critical of the
roles available for women in television drama; as a writer, she was
determined to create roles that featured women in challenging,
unconventional roles. It was unlikely she would have succeeded without
the help of Verity Lambert, executive producer of drama at Thames
Television. Lambert was actively involved in a sustained campaign to
increase opportunities for women in broadcasting, a campaign that
gained momentum in the 1970s following a series of legal victories for
women that granted them the right to equal pay and equal opportunities
with their male competitors in the workplace, the Equal Pay Act (1970)
and the Sex Discrimination Act (1975).

By the mid-1970s it was beginning to be recognised that television,
increasingly a part of everyday life, played a crucial role in the shaping of
social attitudes and identities, including social attitudes towards women
and women's own horizons of expectation. For activists in the broadcasting unions, the issue of equality was central to demands for a wider
range of representations of women *on* the screen that would broaden
these horizons and the kind of opportunities *behind* it that would enable
more women to produce and create a wider range of representations. In
spite of being increasingly well qualified, women working in television
were concentrated primarily in lower-paid service and support jobs;
many campaigned to put an end to outdated working practices that
restricted their opportunities to work as producers, directors, camera
operators and technicians (Ross Muir 1988: 141). They argued that if
there were more women at all levels in broadcast production, more
women would be commissioned to create programmes and more
attention would be given to the development of a rich and varied range
of female role models, an argument that La Plante, frustrated by the lack
of interesting roles for women, fully supported.

Although broadcasters in Britain were thoroughly schooled in their
public-service duties and demonstrated careful of awareness of political
bias, when it came to issues of gender and racial representation they
were deaf and blind. On television, as in most other areas of public life,
women (the majority of the population) and other 'minority' groups
were denied the right to represent themselves not because of policies
that deprived them of access to programme making but because the

paternalistic ethos of Reithian public service – to inform, educate and entertain – that had informed British broadcasting since its inception was sustained by a male elite who assumed that they knew what was of value and therefore 'good' for everybody else (Gallagher 1980; Simms 1985). It took years of campaigning to convince them that people who pay taxes (including the television licence fee) and have the right to vote are entitled to air their own views and opinions on television and to select the programmes they want to watch.

In the wake of the equal-opportunities legislation of the mid-1970s that enabled women to claim equal pay for equal work for the first time, feminist activists began to make themselves heard; they argued that until there were more women in all areas of television production, it was unlikely that women writers, even if they were commissioned, could make any real difference to images of women on the screen. A sustained campaign of action for change began on two fronts, one from within the broadcasting unions demanding more opportunities for women at all levels of the decision-making and production process, the other an educational offensive that aimed to persuade women in general to protest about their representation in the media (King and Stott 1977; Baehr 1980b). Faced with this double offensive, the undeniable fact that women constituted 52 per cent of the population and new laws that gave weight to their claims, the broadcasting institutions had to listen and begin a slow process of change.

The results of an enquiry into the status of women in the film and television industries conducted for the ACTT (Association of Cinematograph, Television and Allied Technicians, now part of BECTU) in 1975 demonstrated conclusively that not only had the position of women in broadcasting not improved since the end of the Second World War (1945), it had actually deteriorated (ACTT 1975). In the 1950s, following their entry into radio broadcasting during the 1940s when many male employees were seconded to operate military communication networks, women worked in a wide variety of occupational grades and constituted 18 per cent of the workforce. By 1975 they constituted 15 per cent and were heavily concentrated in lower-paid service and support roles ghettoised as 'women's work' (Benton 1975). Talking of her time as a researcher and then a producer at Granada in the 1960s and 1970s, Marjorie Giles has described the ways in which her contributions were largely ignored in favour of those made by her male co-workers. The advice from senior management was that if she wanted to be taken seriously, she would have to become 'one of the boys':

The day came when David Plowright called me in and told me I had to change my lifestyle. Spending time drinking with 'the boys' was an important aspect of my job and he advised me to socialise with them after work and become part of the team. It was advice I took to heart: I started going to the New Theatre pub regularly, and later, the Film Exchange became my second home. By the time I retired, I was smoking sixty *Disques Bleu* and drinking half a bottle of Scotch a day. Also, my ladylike manners had also long ago deserted me, and at one stage I even had a memo from Mike Scott complaining about my 'immoderate language'. But by then, I had learnt that if I wanted to get any message across, I had to scream and shout, and make my presence felt. Quiet and reasonable requests got me nowhere. (Giles 2003)[2]

The consequence of this ongoing process of 'masculinisation' of the female members of the workforce was to marginalise women, albeit not an objective that was deliberately pursued. With survival in the industry dependent on women becoming 'one of the boys', it was not surprising to find declining numbers of women in senior creative posts or positions of authority; Verity Lambert at Euston Films was one of the few women to achieve executive status by the late 1970s. Parallel research on media sexism and the representation of women concluded that most of television's output reflected overwhelmingly the values and prejudices of white male middle-class programme makers (Gallagher 1980; Baehr 1981); hence the preponderance of roles that reflected their values, such as the numerous prostitutes La Plante played in crime dramas in the 1970s.

Action for change

Of course we have women in senior management – we all have wives. (broadcasting executive, quoted in Koerber 1977: 127)

The broadcasting unions played a major role in persuading employers to deliver on the equal-opportunities agenda. At this time, British television was still a closed shop; a person who was not a member of a recognised broadcasting union could not be employed. The BBC's ruling on the de-sexing of jobs anticipated the possibility of an anti-discriminatory equal-opportunities bill becoming law in 1975. As a result, most advertised posts encouraged women to apply, but owing to past prejudices there were far too few women with the qualifications and experience to take up many of the positions on offer. Those who did apply felt that they had to prove that they were at least three times better than anyone else applying to do the same job; in practical terms this

meant proving that they were better than men with equivalent qualifications. Substantive accounts of the numbers of women working in
television were collected by the two principal broadcasting unions, the
Association of Broadcast and Allied Staffs (ABS) and the Association of
Cinematograph, Television and Allied Technicians (ACTT), which
organised and represented the interests of production staff such as
directors, writers, floor managers, designers, production assistants and
location managers as well camera and sound crews, editors and
engineers.

The ABS recognised that gender discrimination was, in practice,
hard to combat and in 1975 submitted evidence to the Annan Committee
on broadcasting on the problems of career structures and promotion for
women. The evidence to Annan was based on two surveys by ABS that
cited insufficient action on behalf of broadcasters to create change,
including a lack of in-service training opportunities. The following
extracts from the report broadly summarise the union's views on media
sexism as perceived at the time:

> The BBC plays a leading role in broadcasting and consequently influ-
> ences the opinions and behaviour of most of our society. Its attitude
> towards women's liberation, its presentation of female politicians and
> personalities, its portrayal of women in drama and comedy programmes,
> its use (or non-use) of women as comperes, newsreaders, panellists and
> experts all affect the way society views women and their aspirations ...
>
> Its biased image of women does not necessarily arise from deliberate
> male attempts to patronise or degrade women; it often develops because
> of the unconscious assumptions and prejudices of the mostly male
> directors and producers who work in a largely male atmosphere (e.g.
> film editors, film cameramen, studio technical managers, heads of
> departments) where there are few women to put forward alternative
> views and where these few women are, they are mainly in subordinate
> positions. (ABS evidence to Annan 1975 cited in Koerber 1977: 127)

As the ABS report points out, women operated in the lower echelons of
the industry as production assistants, secretaries, typists, tea ladies,
makeup girls and cleaners. The few who occupied the middle ground as
researchers and script editors had very little control over the material
that they handled and no opportunity to appear on screen presenting it.
In the creative and executive areas, research commissioned by the
ACTT showed that numbers of women were starting to fall as the
women recruited in wartime, when there was a shortage of males,
reached retirement age (ACTT 1975). Even so, most of those in senior
positions tended to be in 'women's' areas such as magazine programmes and children's TV; men were rarely interested in 'women's

issues' and these less prestigious areas were largely ignored by those with serious career ambitions.

The ACTT supported the claims of ABS, submitting evidence that pointed to blatant discrimination in the technical fields and at higher levels of production:

> It is not surprising that men accustomed to working with women filling subordinate roles should automatically and unquestioningly produce programmes which portray women as servers, subjects or objects, as mere appendages to more powerful (and by today's values, more interesting) males and very seldom as individuals in their own right. (ACTT evidence to Annan 1975 cited in Koerber 1977: 127)

The unions recommended introducing quotas to ensure that women were given opportunities to do jobs formerly held only by men; positive discrimination would go some way to redressing the balance and easing the strain on 'lone battlers', those who carried the burden of their gendered identity in a hostile working environment. Other measures proposed by the unions included opportunities for in-service training, the provision of childcare facilities and paid maternity leave. Koerber concludes her assessment of the situation by stating: 'Until women have a voice in the way programmes are made, and what they should be about, we shall continue to see what men *think* women are, not what women *know* they are' (1977: 142). Lambert's awareness of these issues was demonstrated by her commissioning policies once she established herself as head of drama at Thames; the success of 'macho' crime series such as *The Sweeney* enabled her to commission more works featuring women in leading roles, such as the adaptation of the Elspeth Huxley novel *The Flame Trees of Thika* (1981) and La Plante's series *Widows*.

One consequence of broadcasters' paternalism, as feminist activists, commentators and critics began to point out in the 1970s, was that there was a very limited range of images of women on television; numerous accounts provide evidence of the lack of women in positions such as news readers and presenters as well as the stereotypical representations depicted in drama and light entertainment (King and Stott 1977; Tuchman *et al.* 1978). In a key collection of articles on women and the media, for example, Carmel Koerber argues that in drama women performed an assortment of traditional supporting roles such as 'daft dolly birds', 'gossiping housewives' and 'dim devoted mums' (Koerber 1977: 123–42). When women did play leading characters, it was often because they were seen as an exception to these traditional stereotypes, freakish characters singled out for their abnormal unfeminine peculiarities, not as interesting people in their own right. The most adventurous images were found in the British spy series *The Avengers* (ITV 1961–8) where a leather-clad Honour Blackman played secret agent Cathy Gale, dedicated to fighting organised crime alongside the bowler-hatted John Steed (Patrick McNee). She was followed by Diana Rigg's Emma Peel (1965–7) and Linda Thorsen as Tara King, each making their mark as active women able to defend themselves several years before imported North American dramas such as *Star Trek* (BBC 1969–71) and *The Bionic Woman* (ITV 1976–9) depicted similarly adventurous 'strong' women.

Other intrepid investigative women on British and American TV in the 1960s included Sally Lomax (Patricia Mort) of *G.S.5* (ITV 1964), Honey West (Anne Francis) in the US series of the same name, Lottie Dean (Patricia Cutts) in the espionage series *Spyder's Web*, Stefanie Powers as *The Girl from Uncle* (US 1967) and Sharron Mcready (Alexandra Bastedo) of *The Champions* (ITV 1969) (Alsop 1984/5: 16–19). In comparison with other images of women on television these series were ahead of their time, depicting their heroines as martial artists, supersonic astronauts and intrepid cyborgs, characters regarded by many feminist critics as male fantasies, token representations of women 'liberated' in order to serve men and their aggressive, imperialist agendas. In *The Making of Star Trek*, Lieutenant Uhura (Nichelle Nichols) is described as:

> torn between the idea of some day becoming a wife and mother, and a desire to remain in service as a career officer. Her life at present is a battle between her female need for the pleasant routine of Earthbound home and family versus the personal challenge of star-ship life and continued new worlds to conquer. (Stephen E. Whitfield and Gene Roddenberry, *The Making of Star Trek*, cited in Koerber 1977: 252)

Uhura was not only a token woman, but also a token black person in the series: although she appeared regularly on the screen, she said very little and did even less. She had few lines, rarely took decisions, seldom left the flight deck to explore other planets and never had romantic or sexual encounters (Koerber 1977: 252). The only exception to this was an early episode where Uhura and Captain Kirk (William Shatner) share the first inter-racial kiss on US television, a lapse of star ship (and, for the time, television) protocol attributed at the time to 'the influence of alien mind control' (Simpson 2002: 72).[3]

In popular series and serials of the day (westerns, police detective, legal and medical dramas) good nearly always triumphs over evil; men invariably play the baddies, men are always the victors, their closest conspirators and colleagues invariably other males. With the rise in popularity of police action series in the 1970s, active roles for women actually declined. Men have the adventures, fight the important battles, make the important decisions, enforce the laws and protect the innocent and helpless; women, if they appear at all, offer light relief and love interest or play the roles of helpless victims and sex objects, roles offering limited possibilities to La Plante and other female actors. Some viewers, unhappy with this state of affairs, actively demanded better roles for women by writing directly to the programme makers. The female police constable introduced to *Softly Softly: Task Force* (BBC 1970–6), for example, was created in response to appeals from female viewers for a woman to play a more important role in the series, but like Lieutenant Uhura in *Star Trek*, she was seen more than she was heard and there was little development of her character. Rare exceptions to this were found in imported American series such as *Policewoman* (ITV 1974–8), but the attempt to combine recognisably feminine qualities in roles normally associated with macho gun-toting males created significant anomalies in characterisation; 'Sergeant Pepper Anderson (Angie Dickinson) combines the "soft" characteristics – she cries a lot – with the tough ones we normally associate with male TV cops', comments Koerber (1977: 133).

Women of significance appearing regularly in prime-time crime/espionage series in the 1970s were Purdey (played by Joanna Lumley) in the *New Avengers* (ITV 1976–7), McMillan's wife Sally (Susan Saint James) in the imported American crime drama *McMillan and Wife* (ITV 1972–9) and Faye Boswell (Googie Withers), the governor of a women's prison in *Within These Walls* (LWT 1974–8). In *McMillan and Wife* fading 1950s matinee idol Rock Hudson plays a San Francisco police chief with a beautiful, fashionably dressed wife who lures him into investigative work at every opportunity, helps him solve the case and never receives credit for her contribution. In contrast, former British cinema star Googie Withers plays a strait-laced prison governor determined to liberalise an outdated institutional regime in *Within These Walls*; according to Koerber, she becomes in the process 'an earthmother governor of limitless patience, tolerance and understanding' (1977: 135). Boswell lasted three years before Helen Forrester (Katherine Blake) took over, only to be succeeded by Susan Marshall (Sarah Lawson) in 1978. Koerber suggests the series failed 'to rise above banality, perhaps because it tried to be all things to all women' (1977: 135). Although a relative failure in feminist terms, the series attracted a loyal audience and inspired the development of the Australian soap *Prisoner: Cell Block H* (ITV 1979–87). *Prisoner* attracted a dedicated following of around ten million viewers in the mid-1980s, becoming in turn a forerunner of La Plante's sequel to *Widows*, *She's Out* (Cinema Verity/La Plante Productions 1995) and her prison drama *The Governor* (La Plante Productions 1995).

Writing for television

Substantive research into the numbers of women writing for television in the 1970s is thin on the ground. Most of the work is somewhat circumspect and relies on rather basic indicators, such as the names on credits published in viewing magazines such as *Radio Times*. A study of a week of BBC programming conducted in 1979 by Elaine Morgan, for example, indicates that in spite of the broadcasters' ostensible commitment to enacting equal-opportunities policies, only thirteen of the fifty-seven writers credited for features, films, plays, series, documentaries and lectures were women and of these, more than half worked in the 'female ghettos' of children's and educational television. The figures indicate that women contributed only 10 per cent of scripted material for adult viewing on the BBC, with similar proportions for commercial television and radio. Morgan points out that given women's achievements in most other areas of literary production, this was a highly unusual situation that could not be 'explained away' by the hypothesis that 'men are ten times more effective at handling words, creating characters, or inventing plots'; other factors had to be involved (Morgan 1979: 212). These 'other factors' not only created a paucity of women writing for television in general, but as La Plante and other female actors argued, a shortage of dramatic parts for women in anything other than conventional roles supporting male leads as girlfriends, prostitutes, wives and mothers.

La Plante's dramas frequently feature working women, central characters who actively intervene in male-dominated workplaces, often working in institutional settings such as prisons and police stations. Such figures were unknown in 1970s series and serials; prime mid-evening time was dominated by police, crime and espionage series aimed at male viewers. The received wisdom in TV scheduling was that male viewers were the most important consumers of television and that their needs had to be catered for, although by the middle of the decade there were some indications that broadcasters were beginning to acknowledge the female viewer in the early evening slot. *Angels* (BBC1 1975–83), a drama focused on the working lives of student nurses, was one of the first series to tackle issues of gender in the workplace, albeit from the perspective of women working in a traditionally female-dominated profession. The driving force behind the development of the series was the dramatist Paula Milne, then a script editor at the BBC, who was later responsible for creating dramas centred on female characters such as the private detective series *Chandler and Co* (Skreba Films/BBC 1994–5) and the acclaimed serial starring Juliet Stevenson, *The Politician's Wife* (C4 1995).[4]

Popular on British television since the 1950s, medical melodramas invariably concentrated on the activities of caring male doctors; women played the role of nurses, silent handmaidens (angels) who helped and assisted the doctors in their work. *Angels* was the first UK medical series to focus exclusively on the experiences of (mostly female) nurses leaving the (mostly male) medics on the periphery of the action. The initiates, representing a range of feminine identities and differences, develop characterisations which take them beyond the simplistic stereotypes found in popular afternoon serials such as *General Hospital* (ATV 1972– 9). Lauded for its social realism, *Angels* was in many ways a gritty, down-to-earth drama that examined the everyday dilemmas and issues facing nurses and the nursing profession, but it neglected to explore the institutional context of nursing work in any real depth and continued to project nursing as a female-dominated profession at the very time that this ideology was beginning to be eroded. The series quickly established itself as a favourite among female viewers young and old, attracting at its peak more than twelve million viewers because of its strong characterisation, 'feminine' values and positive depiction of the emotional work of caring (Hallam 2000a: 79–81).

Angels helped pave the way for female writers and producers, although it received little attention from feminist critics in spite of innovative approaches to its subject matter; even if they were successful, female creators of television drama remained invisible, their work of marginal interest. Most popular television drama – and soap and series drama in particular – was regarded by the critical (and broadcasting) establishment as a rather mindless form of entertainment, a 'dumbing down' of the cultural values invested in literary forms such as the novel and writing for the stage. Only programmes with 'serious' intent such as current affairs, news, documentaries and drama productions with culturally prestigious literary or theatrical pedigrees were granted sustained critical attention. Highly favoured were portmanteau series such as *Play for Today* (BBC 1 1970–84), a vehicle for the single play that promoted experimental and frequently controversial work by acknowledged and acclaimed writers such as Trevor Griffith, Mike Leigh and Dennis Potter. *Play for Today* had inherited the mantle of prestige from its predecessor *The Wednesday Play* (BBC 1 1964–70), best remembered perhaps for launching the careers of producer Tony Garnett and director Ken Loach. These anthology series were dedicated to producing new works written exclusively for television, much in the way that prestigious theatres such as the Royal Court occasionally devoted a season to promoting the work of new writers for the stage. With television heralded by some critics as 'the largest theatre in the world' (Sutton 1982), the single-play series came to be seen as 'the form most licensed to give an opinion' (Bignell *et al.* 2000: 5). Definitions of authorship and 'quality' in television drama circled around writing for these single-play slots; series and serial drama were considered, at best, popular generic texts that limited experimentation and ran the risk of becoming, to use the words of writer David Edgar, 'aridly self-referential' (Edgar 2000: 77).

Critical interest in the heyday of the single play continues unabated, with archival research throwing light on the commissioning and production processes. Some of this research raises questions about how the ideologies of gender inscribed in the institutions of broadcasting affected the careers of women writers. Drawing on her exploration of the development of the BBC's *Wednesday Play* productions, Madeleine Macmurraugh-Kavanagh argues that the masculinisation of broadcasting was well under way by the 1950s, by which time it was clear that television was not only big business but a medium with previously unimaginable potential for cultural penetration:

> from the moment the material profits and socio-cultural implications of television were fully realised, the broadcasting institutions systematically invented themselves as 'male authorities' (a multi-dimensional tautology), occupying the role of socio-cultural and ideological 'gatekeepers' to a patriarchal hegemonic discourse that was in a permanent state of process. (M. Macmurraugh-Kavanagh 1999: 411)

With television production constructed as an activity primarily for men, television viewers were feminised and assigned the role of passive 'message receivers', a position reinforced in part by the nature of television as a domestic medium and its place in the corner of the living room, in part because the act of consumption itself (of goods, of entertainment) was regarded as an essentially passive, feminine activity excluded from the public sphere of production and creativity (Huyssen 1986; Thumim 2002).[5] The antithesis of consumption, authorship was defined as and associated with maleness; hence Sydney Newman, the founding producer of the single-drama anthology series *Armchair Theatre* (ABC/ITV 1957–9), could order the male writers he commissioned to conceive of the audience as 'a woman to be wooed – and a respectable woman at that' (Newman, quoted in Macmurraugh-Kavanagh 1999: 412).

These gendered discourses of male / active producer and writer, female / passive consumer and viewer were so close to the heart of broadcasting's institutional practices that even critically acclaimed and award-winning female authors such as Fay Weldon found it impossible to command the resources that, by the end of the 1960s, were allocated to male drama writers. Drama, defined as the single play, was considered by its male gatekeepers as a potentially progressive form of programming, able to air contemporary social issues and incorporate new subjects for drama such as working-class characters and (occasionally) other minority voices including those of women. The situation was exacerbated by the shift from studio production to filming on location in the interests of creating the 'realism of record' now associated with two key works of the era, the Tony Garnett and Ken Loach productions *Up the Junction* (BBC 1965) and *Cathy Come Home* (BBC 1966). Both of these television plays, although ostensibly about women's issues (with the former based on a book by a woman) and potentially offering potent roles for female actors seeking to portray women's experiences, objectify their leading female characters. Using 16 mm filming techniques that privileged observational *cinéma vérité* style camerawork in combination with improvised performances and authoritative statistical information presented in voice over, the female actors became the objects of a public (male) gaze, part of a probing social enquiry into the lives of working-class people. The treatment of controversial sociopolitical issues (in the case of *Up the Junction*, that of abortion) using these techniques established a style of drama that aspired to the 'realism of record' found in documentary production; although ostensibly addressed to everyone, the public gaze of these documentary dramas reinforced the viewpoint of those who commanded economic resources and stood behind the camera (Macmurraugh-Kavanagh 1999: 409–25).

Macmurraugh-Kavanagh points out that in debates about the gendering of television drama, the relationship between content and form has a particular significance. The use of documentary strategies to make dramas defined the priorities and pleasures of TV drama as 'male-inscribed in a narrative process which radically excluded female networks of meaning', meanings that embraced levels of emotional affects and engagements, often dismissed by male critics as melodrama. The technique confirmed the treatment of women in male-authored 'opinionated' dramas as objects of detached speculation in tandem with what Macmurraugh-Kavanagh describes as 'a male mediation of "public" reality in definitive terms', a transaction that 'sited both the "standard of writing" and the "top writers" in a determining television genre as unequivocally male' (Macmurraugh-Kavanagh 1999: 423). To become recognised as an author of any significance, female writers had to engage with drama production on these terms; hence Fay Weldon, in spite of a successful track record in writing television dramas that spanned several decades, was told by the BBC that her own adaptation of her novel *The Lives and Loves of a She-Devil* was 'too cruel and too harsh'. Instead, they chose a male writer with a known track record, Ted Willis, to adapt her controversial feminist text. The result is a narrative that focuses on the vengeful fury of a wife who is scorned rather than a narrative that probes the emotional and psychological trauma of rejection. Weldon's own view is that her adaptation was 'less about men, more about women; less about revenge, more about envy'.[6]

For woman writers, exploding male-determined definitions of television authorship and claiming the right to express themselves proved to be more than a matter of demonstrating the 'quality' of their work; the form itself mitigated against expressing what Macmurraugh-Kavanagh terms 'the emotional and psychological level of experience as it is *felt*, rather than experience as it is materially *lived*', a process that effectively excluded them (1999: 418, italics in original). As the voices of women from all walks of life began to rise in protest at their exclusion from public life and demand, amongst other things, the right to control their own bodies and equal pay for equal work, there was actually a decline in the commissioning of women writers for the prestigious *Wednesday Play* slot towards the end of its run. Although women were sometimes commissioned to write one-offs for anthology series and comedy playhouse slots, very few were commissioned to write series or serial drama. One consequence of this exclusion was the lack of a tradition to write in, to feel a part of; every time a drama written by a woman was televised it struggled for critical visibility. Macmurraugh-Kavanagh has pointed out how Julia Jones's *A Bit of a Crucifixion, Father* (1966), a play about a Catholic woman facing yet another unwanted pregnancy televised just prior to the parliamentary debate on the controversial abortion law reform bill, was dismissed as 'melodramatic' by male critics, who preferred the ostensibly more objective account of Loach and Garnett's *Up the Junction* (1966). Even though the book on which the screenplay for *Up the Junction* was based was written and adapted by a woman, Nell Dunn, producer Tony Garnett virtually rewrote the text in partnership with director Ken Loach. According to BBC records, *A Bit of a Crucifixion, Father* was a more successful play with audiences than *Up the Junction*, with ratings in excess of 70 per cent on the BBC's appreciation monitor. In spite of this high level of 'strategic penetration' of the popular audience it is Loach and Garnett's treatment of the issue that received critical acclaim in its day and as a consequence Jones's play has all but disappeared from the history books.

These issues have had long-lasting consequences for female writers, influencing the critical response to La Plante's work and her own defence of her work. Used initially by Trevor Griffith, the term 'strategic penetration' has been used to define 'serious' drama (authored single plays, mini-series and the crime series) from drama that is 'simply television' such as soap. The use of the metaphor is interesting, a further example of the way in which male writers (and critics) regard the television audience in feminine terms (Thornham 2003). The preference for realism and 'objectivity' as a mark of quality and excellence, and abhorrence of melodrama's focus on personal feelings, had a profound effect on women writers, as the account of the production and reception of La Plante's work in the following chapters demonstrates. Squeezed out of the single-play slot, continuing serials provided one of the few opportunities for women writers in the 1970s, their career trajectories shaped by the demands of ensemble writing and serial production. Soap, the most popular genre on television, was regarded by broadcasters as a 'woman's genre' and was therefore one of the few spaces where women writers could air their ideas, with Granada's *Coronation Street* in particular providing opportunities to develop a range of prominent female characters and female-centred storylines. In 1973 Susi Hush, a new young female producer, began to influence the show; she abolished the strict guidelines imposed by her predecessors and placed more emphasis on conflict between the sexes. Plausibly depicting the tension and mutual suspicion between men and women, *Coronation Street* openly aired the problems of those who lived in traditional northern working-class communities. Most of the characters at this time were a cross section of working-class women, many of whom had jobs outside the home. Marion Jordan categorises them as grandmother figures such as Ena Sharples (Violet Carson), Betty Turpin (Betty Driver) and Annie Walker (Doris Speed), mature sexy marriageable women such as Rita Fairclough (Barbara Knox), Elsie Tanner (Pat Phoenix) and Bet Lynch (Julie Goodyear), spinsterly types such as Emily Bishop (Eileen Derbyshire) and Mavis Riley (Thelma Barlow) and young women such as Gail Tilsey (Helen Worth) and Deidre Langton (Anne Kirkbride), some of whom still populate the serial thirty years later (Jordan in Dyer *et al.* 1981: 67–74). Thinkers and activists as well as wives, mothers and girlfriends, these women dominated the street, sometimes wielding their power indirectly through the men.

In contrast ATV's *Crossroads* (1964–88), devised by Hazel Adair and Peter Ling, had comparatively low standards of production, writing and acting but similarly to *Coronation Street* attracted huge audiences to its five times a week early evening slot for much of its twenty-four-year run. Noele Gordon played Meg Richardson, a self-made woman who on the death of her husband turned her West Midlands home into a small hotel, eventually converting it to a motel. A successful business woman, Meg developed a large fan club as she coped with running the motel assisted by her daughter Jill (Jane Rossington) and son Sandy (Roger Tonge) who, following a crippling injury in a road accident, became paraplegic. *Crossroads* centred around the day-to-day problems of the hotel's staff and their families, dealing with emotional issues untouched by other serials of the day, such as the problems of physical and emotional readjustment for a paraplegic, rehousing an elderly couple, abortion and adoption (Hobson 1982). As Koerber (1977) notes, soaps had little appeal for militant women but they were one of the few places on television that offered an ongoing female view of the world and a wide variety of images of women. In this sense they were potential sites for renegotiating femininity and female subjectivities, even though they rarely challenged, in any overt or obvious way, the dominant values and attitudes of the day.

One of the first women to write regularly for television was another Liverpudlian, Carla Lane, one of the few women commissioned in the 1970s and 1980s to write comedy series. If soap is often regarded as a feminine form or a woman's genre, 1970s situation comedy was invariably seen as a bastion of traditional sexist attitudes centred on male characters and patriarchal values (Medhurst and Tuck 1982; Neale and Krutnik 1990). Comedy writing at this time was still an all-male preserve apart from one-off contributions to new talent slots such as *Comedy Playhouse*, although by the end of the decade women writers were gaining ground thanks to Lane's pioneering efforts. Well known for the dizzy, dotty young women in *The Liver Birds* (BBC 1 1969–79) that she created with Myra Taylor, Lane centred her first solo series on a middle-class suburban housewife with grown-up children facing a mid-life crisis. In *Butterflies* (BBC 2 1978–80, 1983) Ria (Wendy Craig) is, as she puts it, 'happily married but not exciting married' to her dentist husband (Geoffrey Palmer) and longs to feel sexually attractive again. She rebels against the 'chains' of her comfortable lifestyle, demands that her husband listens to her feelings of frustration and entrapment and plays with the idea of having an affair. The programme, dubbed by some a 'brief encounter' for the 1970s because of its references to 1940s British films, was much derided by feminists at the time for its middle-class pretentions and Ria's whimsical girlishness, although Ria's insistence that there was more to life than housework and domestic boredom struck chords with many female viewers. In retrospect, it can be seen that Ria's dislike of cooking and her rejection of home life evoked a criticism of suburban married life not dissimilar to that voiced by middle-class American housewives in the 1960s book by Betty Friedan often considered the founding text of second-wave feminism, *The Feminine Mystique*. In interviews Lane rejects the suggestion that she might have had feminist sympathies, although she was well aware of gender prejudice and the problems faced by women writers. Even with her proven track record of writing popular female-centred comedies, it took her three years to persuade the BBC that the theme of potential adultery explored in *Butterflies* could be even remotely funny (Hallam 2005).

In the early 1980s female writers continued to battle with masculine definitions of what might constitute 'quality' and institutionally entrenched views on audience preferences and tastes. Jill Hyem, one of the writers of *Tenko* (1981–4), an award-winning BBC series that focused on the lives of a group of women interned by the Japanese for three and a half years during the Second World War, highlights the problem of realising her ideas in an arena dominated by male decision makers. Like La Plante, Hyem was an actress before she began writing, driven to put pen to paper because of a dearth of good roles for women and a lack of subject matter that reflected a female point of view. In her account of working on *Tenko*, Hyem claims that most of the conflict arose from the different perspectives of the female writers and the male production crews. On the one hand, the writers were constantly warned, 'Don't let's have any *Women's Own* writing'; on the other, bad language was seen as 'unsuitable' for women characters. Dialogue and scenes termed 'unfeminine' were softened; if scripts were left intact, music and lighting were used to romanticise and 'rose tint' scenes intended to be harrowing and stark. Any hint of lesbianism between the all-female occupants of the prison camps was seen as a 'turn off' because characters would lose audience sympathy. After a battle, Hyem was able to depict this aspect of friendship and passion between women, and this led in subsequent series to dealing with important controversial issues such as abortion, euthanasia and suicide (Hyem 1987: 156).

Before writing TV drama, Hyem was warned by other female writers of the 'male mafia' on certain programmes that never employed women writers – in particular, the more expensive crime thrillers and spy genres made on location. Her experiences are similar to those of other female writers in the early 1980s: certain genres – including quality drama and light entertainment – were virtually inaccessible to them. According to Bird and Eliot the 1980s is characterised by male writers moving into the former 'female' territory of children's television; the soaps, even the newer ones, continued to be dominated by male writers but there were no moves by women writers into the male-dominated genres of crime, cops, espionage and thrillers in spite of a growing number of series centred on female professionals such as *Juliet Bravo* and *The Gentle Touch* (Bird and Eliot 1993). Interestingly, they do not mention Lynda La Plante or her first drama, *Widows*, even though she is the first woman to tackle the 'masculine' genre of the crime thriller and 'penetrate' the male-dominated prime-time schedules. It was while playing a prostitute in *The Gentle Touch* and feeling thoroughly frustrated with the role that La Plante first thought of writing the series that became *Widows*, but without the women in charge of production at Thames Television's Euston Films encouraging her to write and helping her to develop the script, it is unlikely *Widows* would have seen the light of day.

Watching *Widows* some twenty years after it was first broadcast, what cannot be recreated (whether seeing it again or for the first time) is the sense of shock and surprise it generated in its day. By placing women at the centre of the action, La Plante turned the generic conventions of the TV crime series inside out. The subject matter was unique for its time: four working-class women plan an armed robbery cross-dressed as men, successfully pull off the job and escape to Brazil with the money! UK television had never screened anything quite like it before. As the audience climbed from eleven million in the first episode to twelve and a half million by the end of the first series, *Widows* was claimed by feminist and non-feminist critics alike as a breakthrough in the representation of women, a decisive intervention in the prestigious all-masculine territory of the crime series. For women working in the broadcasting industry the production of *Widows* and its popular success were an indication that years of exclusion from the creative aspects of production were finally ending; at last a serial written and produced by women had penetrated the consciousness of television executives as well as viewers. The glass ceiling in broadcasting, remorselessly battered by feminist and union activists, had finally cracked; *Widows* was heralded as a sign by seasoned campaigners and critics alike that women behind the screen as well as on the screen could be seen and heard, fully functioning in adult roles.

Notes

1 See, for example, Fay Weldon, *The Life and Loves of a She Devil* (BBC 1986) and *Big Women* (C4 1998); Debbie Horsefield, *Making Out* (BBC 1989–91) and *Cutting It* (BBC 2003–4); Lucy Gannon, *Soldier, Soldier* (ITV 1991–7), *Peak Practice* (ITV 1993–2001) and *Bramwell* (ITV 1995–8); Kay Mellor, *Band of Gold* (ITV 1995–7), *Playing the Field* (ITV 1998–2000) and *Fat Friends* (ITV 2002–).

2 This comment is taken from the draft typescript of Giles's account of working at Granada; it is omitted from the published account. See Giles in Finch, Cox and Giles 2003: 38–42.

3 For a more detailed account of racialised representation on early US television see, for example, Haralovich 1999.

4 Milne's credits include episodes of *Coronation Street, Crossroads, Z Cars, Juliet Bravo* and *The Ruth Rendell Mysteries* and serials *The Fragile Heart, A Bunch of Fives* and *The Hollow Reed,* as well as a number of stage plays.

5 For further development of this argument in the American context see Spigel and Mann 1992.

6 Fay Weldon in conversation with Julia Hallam at 'On the boundary: turning points in TV drama 1965–2000', conference at the University of Reading, 3–5 April 1998.

Writing, acting, power

2

> I think one of reasons that *Widows* was as successful as it was, was that it was the first time women – real women, if you like – were in the front, driving it on, casting the right way, looking the right way. And written the right way. (Linda Agran in Alvarado and Stewart 1985: 107)

Old television dramas often reveal their artifice and construction in ways that make them boring and predictable for contemporary viewers. Ensemble casts, shorter sequencing and an increase in the pace of editing tend to proliferate in multi-channel environments; modern dramas are less about character development and more about stars, less about words and more about spectacle (Nelson 1997). By comparison, 'old' series and serials can seem slow and stilted, the emphasis on script-led camerawork creating a rather static image, the lack of overt stylisation a rather dull form of generic realism often dubbed 'naturalism' by its critics (Caughie 2000a). *Widows* is something of an exception to much of the drama of this type produced in the early 1980s; it plays homage to the British crime thriller and American *film noir* of the 1940s and 1950s, taking the action-based heist film as its generic template. The decision to shoot on film rather than video allowed for greater fluidity of camera movement, contributing to what was regarded at the time as a distinctively 'modern' form of generic realism, but primarily it was the focus on women as central characters that situates *Widows* as a unique contribution to the UK crime serial, heralding the arrival of women as characters who lead the action rather than playing roles where they are cast as sexy appendages to male protagonists.

Gender, genre, *Widows*

In the early 1980s, Verity Lambert, head of drama at Thames Television, was one of the few women in the industry to have reached a position where she controlled the commissioning process. Lambert began her TV career at ABC in the 1950s working as a production assistant with Sydney Newman, originator of the groundbreaking (in its day) *Armchair Theatre* series that produced new plays written especially for television. When he moved to the BBC as head of drama and started *The Wednesday Play*, he offered Lambert the opportunity to produce a new science-fiction series called *Doctor Who*. The series ran for twenty-six years, with Lambert playing a significant role in building its success before leaving to produce *Adam Adamant Lives* (BBC 1 1966–7) (Tulloch and Alvarado 1983: 16–57). She joined Thames shortly afterwards to produce *Budgie* (ITV 1971–2), briefly returning to the BBC before becoming head of drama at Thames Television and executive producer at their off-shoot drama production unit Euston Films.

Thames Television was the largest and wealthiest of the independent broadcasting companies that formed the ITV network in the 1970s; the other networking companies at this time were Central, Granada, London Weekend and Yorkshire, supplemented by a number of regional companies that included Anglia, Border, Grampian, HTV, Scottish, TV South, TV South West, Tyneside and Ulster.[1] Thames TV set up Euston Films and registered it as a subsidiary in 1971 to make drama on film for the ITV network; the idea was that it would enable films to be made for television on a freelance, non-capital expenditure basis by operating with a minimum number of permanent administrative staff. The following account of the company's ethos and practice and the development of La Plante's first serial *Widows* is drawn from Manuel Alvarado and Stewart's extensive research documented in *Made for Television: Euston Films Limited* (1985). Euston incorporated the ethos of a small film studio with the practicalities of making modestly budget productions for television, a combination that played a major role in defining 'the look' and style of their TV series. The initial series of films made for television was dubbed *Armchair Cinema* in homage to the prestige of the single play. The agenda at Euston, however, was not to innovate formally or introduce contentious new work; it was to make TV movies that would act as pilots for subsequent series and action series. Euston's most successful series *The Sweeney* (Thames/Euston Films 1975–8), created by Ian Kennedy Martin, was a spin-off from *Regan*, a ninety-minute film developed for the *Armchair Cinema* slot under Euston's initial remit of making films for television. When Jeremy Isaacs took over as programme controller at Thames, he wanted a hit series; *The Sweeney* provided it, with Verity Lambert taking over as controller of drama shortly before the first series was transmitted. The success of *The Sweeney* gave Lambert freedom to commission more 'risky' productions such as *Rock Follies* (Thames 1976–7) by Howard Schuman, based on the adventures of an all-female rock band, and *Bill Brand* (Thames 1976), a left-wing political drama by Trevor Griffiths.

One of the first dramas Lambert commissioned to be made at Euston was *Out* (Thames/Euston Films 1978), written by Trevor Preston. This series, a revenge narrative centred on a convicted bank robber, and its partner *Fox* (Thames/Euston 1980), a family saga of working-class London life, provided a model of sorts for *Widows*. Another of Lambert's projects, *The Flame Trees of Thika* (Thames/Euston Films 1981), a serialisation of a book by Elspeth Huxley, offered a white child's view of going to Kenya with her parents in 1918 to start a new life as coffee planters. Lambert thought Euston a very male-orientated company; this series, focused on strong, courageous women, was a change from 'the rather macho stuff' that they were making at that time. She regarded *Thika* as 'a feminist story, one in which the women are the ones who get things done and come to terms with their lives'. Following its transmission, a number of feminist friends made Lambert far more conscious 'of the fact I really should try and do something about women. Which is how – well when *Widows* came in I was very specifically trying to look for something that had women as the protagonists as opposed to men' (Lambert in Alvarado and Stewart 1985: 105).

Linda Agran shared Lambert's views on the paucity of roles for women and recognised in La Plante's ideas the kind of drama they were looking for:

> Lynda came in with an idea which she claimed she couldn't write. She said it's a six-parter and outlined it. She's an actress who has written little bits and bobs but certainly nothing as ambitious as this. And she said she could probably write the first one but after that she wasn't sure. So I said, well I'll commission the first script and if it's any good I'll commission the remaining five. And you'll have to do it unless you want to be really embarrassed and start returning the money. So that's exactly what happened. (Alvarado and Stewart 1985: 107)

Asked about the attitude of the Thames hierarchy to the project, Agran replied:

> 'Well, first of all they don't read scripts. And I can get quite angry about the fact that they're either buying my judgement or they are not. Other people's views of scripts are interesting but they are not going to affect my view of them. So when I told them about *Widows* they were in fact very supportive about the idea. I softened it a bit, but they saw it as a sort of crime thriller/ mystery/ twist and turn story and they felt there was

some strength to my argument, I think, that women are not seen as often as they should be on television and not in the right roles. So there was a fair amount of enthusiasm for it. (Alvarado and Stewart 1985: 108)

Asked about the experience of working on a female-controlled production and whether this might alter the representation of the women on the screen, Agran commented:

I really think that it needs a woman, not necessarily a woman producer, but it needed a woman there all the time in terms of casting, attitudes, in terms of the women's attitudes to each other, and so I decided to produce it myself. Well, I'm delighted with the success and I'm pleased that I did it. It was a real labour of love, though; I enjoyed doing it. It was also lovely casting blokes to do bits on the side. I used to fantasise with Lynda about having casting sessions with blokes – telling them to take their clothes off, you know – but of course we didn't do any of that! (Alvarado and Stewart 1985: 106–7)

Agran's response supports the claims made by feminist critics and activists, that changes in the representation of women could only be achieved if women are involved at all levels in the production process, but has an interesting caveat:

You see, the problem with series writing, and the problem with a lot of differences between men and women and the way they're perceived and the way they're portrayed, is that male writers can't write women – or think they can't, so they tend to avoid writing them ... [It's] Almost as though [they're] dealing with Martians. Men, because they don't want to get it wrong, leave them out. (Alvarado and Stewart 1985: 107–8)

Given a long history in literature and drama of men writing about women and creating female characters, Agran's comments here seem a little ingenuous.

Lambert articulates a greater awareness of the difficulties of producing work written by or focused on women; a major problem was convincing the executive hierarchy that such programmes could achieve the kind of high viewing figures deemed essential for company prestige and status as well as economic survival. There was a general consensus in the industry that evening viewing was still controlled by the senior male in a household; once he returned from work, he would choose what was watched and it was his taste that was given the greatest consideration by the broadcasting companies. Hence, soaps were shown in the afternoon or early in the evening, their repetitive structures and ongoing storylines designed to engage the 'distracted' attention of the female viewer as she tended to her household duties (Modleski 1982). Prime time was reserved for programmes regarded as 'serious interest'

with news, documentary and current affairs, and 'quality' entertainment in the form of action and crime series, dominating the schedules.
Ethnographic research of viewing activity in the home tended to support
this view; Morley (1986), for example, found that male heads of
households usually controlled what was watched by the family in the
evening. Professional socialisation instilled similar views amongst
production staff, as this comment by director Ian Toynton reveals:

> It was very strange on *Widows* too because when I was working on it right
> at the beginning people used to say, 'Oh, it's about women. Nah, won't
> work, people won't watch it'. – 'Who won't watch it?' And they would say,
> 'Well, women won't watch it because they won't be interested enough
> and it will turn men off because they won't want to watch a lot of heavy
> dykes holding up a ...' And it was interesting that they were proved to be
> absolutely wrong. Women loved it. (Alvarado and Stewart 1985: 108)

Given male control of prime-time viewing in the home and the high
viewing figures, it seems that men loved it too.

Reinventing the crime thriller

The enormous success of *Widows* was a surprise to industry
professionals and critics alike. Popular crime series such as *The Sweeney*
and *The Professionals* were typically centred on male cops and their
action-orientated criminal-catching capers, with point of view and the
moral high ground firmly positioned with the police. In the 1970s *The
Sweeney* was praised as one of the most believable police series on
television; based on the activities of the Flying Squad, an elite corps of
the Metropolitan Police ('Sweeney Todd' is cockney rhyming slang for
Flying Squad), the series focused on Detective Chief Inspector Jack Regan
(memorably played by John Thaw), an old-fashioned individualist who
solves crimes through a mixture of intuition and bullying, techniques
increasingly at odds with the more bureaucratic, scientific methods of
modern policing favoured by his superiors. Regan has similarities to
other anomic male heroes found in the *films noirs* of an earlier
generation as well as popular contemporaneous American detectives in
series such as *Kojak* (US Universal, BBC 1 1974–8) and *Starsky and
Hutch* (US Spelling-Goldberg, BBC 1 1976–81). Separated from his
wife, alienated from his superiors, cynical and world weary with only a
young rookie for comradeship (Detective Sergeant Carter, played by
Dennis Waterman), Regan fights crime on the streets with the intensity
of a vigilante. Cultural analysts regarded the popularity of these violent

crusading lawmen as indicative of wider feelings of alienation and helplessness in a society perceived by many as increasingly out of control, corrupted by organised crime, big business and dishonest politicians. Leon Hunt, for example, describes how the feeling that the 1970s had become a more frightening time than previous decades can be found across a wide range of cultural indicators including press reports, political discourse, popular music and bestselling novels. Anxious citizens were worried that the UK was becoming anarchic and 'ungovernable', a perception fed by increases in trade-union and student militancy, the trials of the vicious Kray, Richardson and Tibbs gangs for their involvement in pornography and racketeering, threats of terrorism and the emergence of street 'mugging' (Hunt 2003: 137–8). Confirmation of these anxieties and perceptions was provided by a breakdown of law and order within the police themselves; there were five major charges of police corruption in the decade, including one against Scotland Yard's Obscene Publications Squad. The in-coming conservative government led by Margaret Thatcher capitalised on people's fears, increasing the power of the police and passing new legislation to limit picketing by strikers, prevent terrorism and curb immigration (Hall *et al.* 1978).

Given the turmoil of the decade, it is unsurprising that contemporary urban life (and the metropolis in particular) provided inspiration for many UK crime films and TV series made in the 1970s. Gangster themes dominated the crime thriller on the big screen: protection and racketeering in *Performance* (1970) and *Get Carter* (1971), gang warfare and conspiracy in *Brannigan* (1975) and *Sweeney!* (1977), and robbery in *The Fast Kill* (1972), *The Squeeze* (1977) and *Sweeney 2* (1978). By the end of the decade, DCI Regan's personal vendetta in *The Sweeney* was analysed as a cry of frustrated rage, the desire to actually do something to improve the status quo channelled into action against those most easily singled out as scapegoats for what is wrong with society, in *The Sweeney's* case primarily petty criminals and minor racketeers (Buscombe 1976: 68). The vigilante detective embodied the helplessness of the ordinary citizen faced with a world he feels he can longer control (Hurd 1981: 53–70). By way of contrast, high-profile press coverage of the escape and capture of violent armed robbers such as John McVicar and the Great Train Robber Ronald Biggs sensationalised their extravagant lifestyles, constructing them as cult heroes and turning them into popular celebrities.

Widows draws on similar themes of gang warfare, armed robbery and extravagant criminal lifestyles but with a unique shift in focus now considered a trademark of La Plante's style: the reversal of gender roles.

La Plante reinvented the crime thriller by creating fresh variations in its structure through a focus on women and their stories; the episodic, hero-centred structure of the crime series was replaced with what Euston producers regarded as the equivalent to a television novel, the ensemble serial. When their husbands are killed committing armed robbery, instead of becoming victims of gang warfare or police harassment the Widows take destiny into their own hands and become robbers themselves. In the early 1980s, such role reversals were unheard of on television; attempts were being made to introduce a feminine perspective into the police series through dramas such as *Juliet Bravo* and *The Gentle Touch*, but *Widows* went further. Not only are women the centre of the drama, they are also in charge of their own lives, arbiters of their own destinies and not 'in service' to any higher authority. It was not just a case of altering the point of view from which the audience experiences the unfolding drama; *Widows* opened up the structure of the crime series by moving it beyond what David Edgar refers to as the 'arid self-referentiality' of generic drama, and by doing so called into question the very conventions on which such definitions and judgements are based. At the same time the genre's most integral aspect, that of generating of suspense and surprise, was enhanced by the change from series to serial format. Instead of the usual episodic structure that critics of day argued provided audiences with satisfying closure and reassurance (Hurd 1981), the serial's ongoing narrative and the introduction of a cliffhanger at the end of each week's hourly episode attracted, maintained and generated a dedicated viewing public. The success of *Widows* was unusual because it was one of the few episodic dramas to build an audience; as the plot developed and became ever more complicated, week by week the serial rose in the ratings. However implausible the basic premise may have seemed initially, increasing numbers of viewers tuned in, eager to discover if the women could not only plan and execute an armed robbery but actually succeed and get away with it.

The plot of *Widows* is a good deal more complicated than was often the case in generic television drama at this time, giving some substance to Euston's claims for the serial's novelistic ambitions – claims given added weight by La Plante's subsequent success as a bestselling novelist. Agran talks about the difficulties of shaping La Plante's material into the six blocks demanded by the schedule, which was ring fenced on one side by *News at 10* and on the other by the requirements of the watershed. This left an hour of prime-time viewing, which, allowing for advertising, had to be shaped into sections amounting to fifty-two minutes in total.

First one came in, terrific, great energy but would have run for about two hours. Realised if I held her up asking for rewrites, because it's got quite a complicated structure, she would have to go back to the beginning again and would probably get lost, so as the first drafts came in, I would ring her about an hour and a half later and say 'terrific, terrific, keep going', and she did. When she'd worked it right through we had this huge file; then I said, 'Right, now we'll start again', so she and I virtually locked ourselves away and went through it and I remember picking up the phone in the middle of night and saying, 'Listen, how the hell did Harry know, etc.' because it really is quite complicated. (Agran in Alvarado and Stewart 1985: 106)

The serial opens with a failed robbery; one man manages to escape the conflagration in the tunnel that follows the armed hold-up of a security van, the others burn to death. Following the incident, the police suspect the Rawlins gang and mount a search operation for the man that escaped. Harry Rawlins's chief adversaries are not the police, however, but another local gang who want to take over his patch, the Fisher Brothers. Instead of the oppositional 'cops and robbers' structure of conventional crime series, the plot has a more complex tripartite configuration of players that includes the widows of the dead men, the Fisher Brothers (who want the dead Harry Rawlins's contact books) and the police. Parallel cross-cutting counterpoints the different organisational strategies of the three groups: the more co-operative structure of the meetings between the women, the hierarchical organisation of the police and the aggressive bullying tactics of the Fisher Brothers. As the plot progresses a number of narrative arcs develop across the serial's ongoing structure and the groups change. When Dolly Rawlins (Ann Mitchell) finds her dead husband's ledgers and his plans for the next armed robbery in his safety deposit box at the bank she decides to attempt the next job herself, persuading the other two Widows, Shirley (Fiona Hendley) and Linda (Maureen O'Farrell), to become her accomplices. The oldest of the three, Dolly assumes an authoritative stance that is by turns cold and manipulative, affectionate and matriarchal. In contrast, Detective Chief Inspector Resnick, convinced that Harry is still alive, begins the serial as a rational, career-orientated detective; as the plot develops and his prey become ever more elusive he becomes fanatical to the point of hysteria. Told by his superior officer to drop the case, he refuses and is suspended from duty. An alienated, lonely figure, he becomes the archetypal 1940s *film noir* private detective as he continues to pursue the criminals in his own time. The Fisher Brothers too are dangerously obsessed by the Widows; thwarted by their failure to persuade Dolly to hand over Harry's ledgers, they become increasingly abusive and violent in their attempts to extract information from Shirley and Lynda. The relative composure of the women (and Dolly in particular) in the face of mounting pressure from all sides stands in marked contrast to Resnick's growing obsession with the case and the escalating violence caused by the Fisher Brothers (whose relationship with each other projects homosexual undertones in an obvious reference to the notorious 1960s East End gangsters the Kray twins).

From the outset, the structure of the serial places the viewer in a position of superior knowledge to the police and detectives who are usually the source of viewer alignment and information. It becomes obvious that neither the police nor the Fisher gang pose any real threat to the Widows as long as they do as Dolly says, try to remain calm and support each other. The all-male police team, far from controlling the action, become the serial's fall guys; unable to enter the gendered spaces where the women meet (the sauna, a women's public toilet), they are left holding the metaphorical baby in the form of Dolly's pet poodle while she plans the next stage of the robbery with Linda and Shirley. In episode three, as the women rehearse their roles at a disused quarry, the presence of a third interest group becomes apparent. A black and white sequence of Harry and his men preparing for the raid is cross-cut with the women practising the same moves; it reveals that, like Dolly, Harry was too slow to make the final run and had to drive the bread truck, the only vehicle to escape the conflagration in the tunnel. We now know that Harry is the unseen presence who has been hiding in the dark corners of the lock-up garage where the women meet and spying on them. The suspense intensifies as Dolly becomes aware that Harry is alive and monitoring their activities, a potential threat to their plans that she will have to deal with.

Through its focus on women as active protagonists in an all-male world, *Widows* offers a very different imaginary to the nostalgic images of working-class femininity found in soaps of the day such as *Coronation Street*, which foreground women's role in the home. Rejecting this focus on the domestic and private sphere, *Widows* foregrounds the women's ability to operate in the public realm as professionals, a status position only conferred in the television world of the time on middle-class women (and, as previously pointed out, very rarely at that). Between them, the four women perform a range of identities commonly associated with representations of working-class women: respectable (and respected) matriarch (Dolly), rebellious wild child (Linda), dizzy dolly bird (Shirley), and a tough former prostitute and exotic dancer (Linda's friend Bella). By depicting these women as characters who refuse to be victims of circumstances, who take control of their own lives, *Widows* offers a strong and liberating image of working-class women in a genre where they were invariably depicted as male appendages, girlfriends, prostitutes and 'absent' wives.

Critical evaluations of the works produced by Euston Films, particularly the more experimental works such as *Fox* and *Minder*, have commented on the rich generic interplay in these works, a generic interplay also present in *Widows*. La Plante was well acquainted with Euston's output, having played minor roles in *The Sweeney*, *Fox* and *Out*. On a more practical level, Euston 'style' combined techniques of film production with television expertise; some of the people who worked at Euston were trained in feature-film production, including Ian Toynton, the director of *Widows*, who was a former assistant editor. Other technical staff and directors came from television, where achieving excellence within the constraints of tight budgeting dominated the ethos of professional practice and notions of 'quality' in British television (Brunsdon 1990). Together, these factors created dramas that looked significantly different in their day. Shooting, usually with 16 mm cameras and radio microphones used in news production, enabled sound and vision to be recorded together on location rather than, as was more common, post-synchronising dialogue re-recorded by the cast in the studio. This created a sense of immediacy and spontaneity often missing from dubbed sound, accentuating the sense of 'liveness' and documentary actuality associated with television realism that, in the wake of the 'realism of record' of the 1960s, continued to define 'quality' popular drama. *Special Branch*, *The Sweeney* and *Minder* were distinguished by psychologically plausible characters moving amidst recognisably contemporary surroundings, with considerable attention paid to authenticity of dialogue and accent although not all Euston productions aimed for this type of realism. *Out*, *Fox* and *Widows* were notably different, drawing on filmic rather than televisual conventions to establish a distinctly fictional generic mood that – like the films made by Euston for theatrical release, *Sweeney!* (1977) and *Sweeney 2* (1978) – paid homage to the British crime thriller.

Out, *Fox* and *Widows* were distinctively 'London' productions that focused on the development of characters through serial (rather than series) form, enabling the creation of more complex characters within multi-faceted fictional worlds. The focus on character shifts the terrain of these serials from a type of realism rooted in the use of location camerawork and authentic dialogue (a realism of street-wise recognitions based on assessments of plausible character motivations, situations and events) to a realism of character rooted in the depiction of psychological and emotional states which relies on a more overt, expressionistic visual style and a heightened level of performance associated with melodrama. In the crime thriller, if the hero is an alienated individual seduced by a *femme fatale* in a moody, expressionistic setting, the thriller is likely to be dubbed a *film noir* (see, for example, Kaplan [1978] 1998 and Krutnik 1991). *Widows* combines the realism of familiar and recognisable locations and characters with aspects of *noir* expressionism and melo-drama to create a psychological portrait that depicts the Widows as women who, in spite of their sorrow and their circumstances, are determined to survive. Whereas women in TV crime series played minor roles of little or no narrative significance, in crime films women are frequently seen as duplicitous and not to be trusted, a theme taken to extremes in *film noir*, where women are often depicted as wicked seducers, *femmes fatales*, who seal the fate of their male hero victims by entangling them in webs of sexual desire, intrigue and murder. In homage to this cinematic heritage, at one point the dialogue of *Widows* makes explicit reference to the star of several well-known 1940s *films noirs*. Watching the widowed Dolly as she approaches them for their first meeting, Linda says to Shirley of the older woman, 'Lana Turner is alive and well and living in St John's Wood', the choice of Turner here perhaps a reference to her highly publicised affair with Los Angeles gangster Johnny Stompanato. In a classic *noir* thriller such as *The Big Heat* (Lang US 1953) the girlfriend of a mobster becomes the *femme fatale* who ensures his downfall. Similarly to this classic depiction of a *noir* spider woman, Dolly will ultimately kill her mate, but not before her ability to deceive and disguise herself has hastened the downfall of Detective Inspector Resnick, the one policeman convinced that her husband is still alive and determined to catch him.

Actor Ann Mitchell and director Ian Toynton wanted to bring to Dolly's character something of the charisma of a *film noir* heroine, but because she is an older woman and the narrative centres on her criminal activities rather than the use of her sexual power, Dolly is no *femme fatale* in any straightforward generic sense. With her blonde hair and forties-style mackintosh belted tightly at the waist, Dolly combines both feminine and masculine aspects of the *noir femme fatale* and her alter ego the male investigator. This androgyny is accentuated by Mitchell's acting, which ranges from an affectionate, nurturing manner towards her poodle to the staccato gestures of her aggressive cigarette smoking and the self-assertive confidence of her purposeful walk. The bleaker aspects of her lonely world are pushed to the margins, hinted at in the operatic elegies she listens to alone at home, the subdued grey greens of the night-time sequences when she walks her dog, and in the garage scenes, where the darkness is punctured by the starkness of the hanging ceiling lights, the silence by the tap-tap-tapping of Dolly's stiletto heels. The ambiguity of her character is accentuated by elements of expressionist cinematography that periodically illuminate her emotional state of mind. In the garage sequences, for example, this is achieved visually through the use of non-standard lenses, low-key lighting, off-centre shot composition and camera angles, all considered typical of *film noir*'s visual style (Place and Peterson [1974] 1996). When she first enters the garage, she is depicted as a tiny figure at the back right-hand corner of the frame, the foreground filled with dark undecipherable shapes. Shooting her movements through a metal grill as she tentatively explores the space and enters the office, the voyeuristic camerawork accentuates feelings of entrapment and vulnerability. In line with this more expressionistic approach, the standard camera rhetoric of television melodrama is largely absent; in particular, there are few close-ups of actors' faces to emphasise emotional response. For the most part, the camera remains at a respectable distance from the face, favouring head and shoulder and mid shots that give the actors space to use their bodies as well as their facial muscles.

As the story progresses, Dolly's air of vulnerability disappears; she moves ever more confidently into the generic space usually occupied by the male lead as she steps into the life of crime left to her by the ostensibly dead Harry. The oldest and most senior of the Widows, Dolly is elegant and dignified, her power as the wife of a 'respected' gangster dependent on a tightly controlled performance that makes others react to her. Dolly maintains a carefully constructed facade of bourgeois respectability; she lives in a large detached house, wears smart fashionable clothes, drinks fine wine and likes opera – tastes associated with wealthy middle-class lifestyles. She sustains this masquerade for much of the time, rarely dropping her façade except on the odd occasion when she expresses her feelings to the other Widows. When the women meet for the first time in the sauna, the warm colour of the wooden interior accentuated by the yellow glow of the lighting is in marked contrast to the stark greyness of earlier sequences drained of colour. In the intense heat of this artificial environment, the Widows vent their emotions and share their grief; even Dolly's tough shell cracks as she cries and then laughs with Linda and Shirley. Dolly's softer, maternal side is glimpsed at odd moments, when she listens to Kathleen Ferrier singing, for example, or offers to prepare some food for her husband's ex-gang member Boxer. The rest of the time, she resists emotional engagement; rigidly controlling any expressive resonance, her voice remains flat and even, her expression tightly controlled and unsmiling.

In interviews actor Ann Mitchell talks at length about how she wanted to explore the ways in which women subject themselves to others and take on a secondary role, a role of service, and yet possess qualities of leadership that are never realised. The air of ambiguity that surrounds Dolly, her tough exterior masking an inner loneliness and vulnerability, is a vital aspect of her character, something Mitchell worked hard to achieve. Mitchell wanted to create someone who was a London woman and who was quite cold and repressed:

> She is unable/refuses to grieve, she is childless and a woman conscious of the loss of her youth amongst people much younger than herself. She has lots of conflicting facets; she alternately negates and embraces maternal feelings; she wants to be beautified and she wants to stay hard. My image of her is that if you touched her she'd break. (Mitchell in Campbell 1985: 13)

Dolly has the ability to pass, to operate in the world, out of the ghetto, anywhere; this sense of being able to pass in middle-class society, not to be exiled from it, was crucial to Mitchell's interpretation of the character. Beatrix Campbell refers to this complex portrayal of a working-class East End London woman as 'an outlaw with class' (1985: 13).

Born into a working-class East End family, Mitchell played Dolly partly with the objective of 'put[ting] the record straight' about those she grew up with and loved; Widows was something of a mission, an opportunity to put right television's representation of the working class. She spent her childhood amongst 'fantastically gifted women' and the memory of their dignity is still strong in her own sense of self-worth. As a child, she went to the cinema about five times a week with her mother and grew up watching movies in which working-class people were invariably portrayed by middle-class actors, usually as comic characters:

> I was brought up with the habit of working-class people being trivialised … working-class speech and locations have become synonymous with violence, lack of intelligence and criminality. That is the cliché about the East End. The reality was very different. My parents were very concerned about education. I'm a beneficiary of the 1944 Education Act. My stepfather, who was a Communist at the time, had a tremendous interest in the world, in politics and culture … The middle-class theory goes that the working classes don't have culture. One of the reviewers of Widows complained that working-class people wouldn't listen to the Kathleen Ferrier theme music. My grandmother was always playing it. (Mitchell in Campbell 1985: 13)

Mitchell had little first-hand knowledge of criminality but brought to the part of Dolly her feelings about economic and emotional deprivation:

I deliberately chose a strong cockney accent to counterpose it with an image that was about style, good taste, about being smart. There's a tremendous premium on that where I come from ... You could pass between classes if you dressed well. There's a love of beauty, line and form. It's my heritage, a sense of the classic. (Mitchell in Campbell 1985: 13)

Mitchell began her dramatic career at the E15 acting school, working with the renowned theatre director Joan Littlewood; other notable actors who trained and worked with Littlewood are Barbara Windsor and Richard Harris. A highly controversial figure in British theatre, Littlewood championed actors from working-class backgrounds at a time when the theatre was still an almost exclusively middle-class institution. Many of the actors trained by Littlewood went on to work in British television in the 1960s when writers and directors such as Troy Kennedy Martin and Ken Loach were busy blurring the boundaries between fact and fiction in realist police series and drama documentaries such as *Z Cars* and *Cathy Come Home* (Lacey 2005). Mitchell began her career in *Z Cars* and then starred in a drama series written by John McGrath and Troy Kennedy Martin and directed by Ken Loach, *The Diary of a Young Man* (BBC 1964), considered by some critics one of the most formally adventurous television dramas of the period (Caughie 2000a: 93). She first met Ian Toynton when she was invited by him to audition for a part in the BBC series *The Chinese Detective* and was offered the part but rejected it because she only had to speak five lines: 'something inside me clicked, I found myself saying no, I told him that, at my age, and after all the years I'd done in the business, I was worth more than that' (Mitchell in Edgecombe 1985: 16). Toynton remembered her when the time came to cast Dolly, and it is as Dolly in *Widows* and the subsequent series, *Widows 2* (ITV 1985) and *She's Out* (ITV 1995), that she found her greatest television success. For Mitchell, the key to the role, as befits her background and training, was to move away from the well-worn clichés associated with working-class women: 'You have choices as an actor and you can choose to express it in a way that is internally truthful and externally interesting' (Mitchell in Campbell 1985: 13).

It is this relationship between internal truth and outward expression that informs the authenticity of Mitchell's award-winning performance.[2] In television drama, powerful performances are dependent upon actors' fundamental ability and freedom to express themselves, a freedom highly dependent upon camerawork and editing. The power of Mitchell's performance depends ultimately not only on a well-written script that conveys plausible character motivation and emotions but on a sympathetic

Widows, ITV (Thames) 1983 [*cont. p. 49*
Dolly Rawlins – Ann Mitchell, Linda Perelli – Maureen O'Farrell, Shirley Miller – Fiona Hendley, Bella O'Reilly – Eva Mottley. Directed by Ian Toynton

rapport between actor, director and production crew. Limitations on an actor's movements and what can be conveyed depend, initially, on camerawork, lighting and framing; the focal length of a shot determines who or what is in focus, and the framing of the body in space reinforces paralinguistic features of performance, such as gestures, body movement and the look (Skirrow 1987: 164).

The relationship between camerawork and acting is brought to the fore in the scene where Linda introduces Bella to Dolly as the potential fourth 'man' in the gang at the end of episode two. Called to an emergency meeting at the garage, Dolly is initially concerned for Linda's welfare; when Dolly realises Linda is drunk, a heated exchange breaks out between the three women that is framed in a shot- reverse-shot sequence using mid and head and shoulder shots of their bodies.

The camerawork accentuates the power relations between the women and their changing attitudes to each other as the sequence develops. In Figure 1, Dolly fills the centre of the screen, hands on hips, as Linda introduces her to Bella, pleading with Dolly to acknowledge Bella's presence (Figure 2). Bella listens to the heated exchange (Figure 3), masculinised not only by her grey mackintosh and short hair but by the way she holds her cigarette between thumb and forefinger. As the emotion intensifies between Dolly and Linda, the camera moves in a little to show Linda's response to Dolly's anger (Figure 4), cutting back to show Linda caught between Bella and Dolly (Figure 5). With their heads and shoulders in the frame, the actors use their bodies as well as their faces to convey initial distrust and combativeness. In the remaining shots in the sequence, the angles of the women's shoulders reflect their reactions to each other, with Bella initially walking away from Dolly (Figure 6) and then turning to face her (Figure 8) once Dolly accepts her (Figure 7). The gradual change in attitudes is conveyed by softening the physical planes of the body in the frame; the shoulders turn with the face towards the camera or the other character, indicating a lowering of guard and growing mutual respect. Throughout this sequence Dolly is weighing up Bella, just as Bella is weighing up Dolly. Their assessment of each other has little in common with conventional depictions of women as judging each other by superficial aspects of appearance such as makeup and fashionable clothes, or their status positions as wives and mothers. Dolly's judgement of Bella is based on her ability to stand up for herself, her self-assurance, confidence and sense of humour, displayed by yet another veiled reference to a classic *film noir* (this time British) when Bella replies to the last of Dolly's questions, 'I drive – and I play a mean tune on the harmonica'. (In *The Third Man* (Carol Reed 1949) the harmonica is associated with the appearance of the enigmatic 'third man' following the funeral of racketeer Harry Lime (Orson Welles).)

Skirrow (1987) argues that the notion of gender as performance is foregrounded in *Widows*. Central to the plot is the ability of the women to impersonate men; it is crucial to their success that as robbers they are mistaken for men, so they have to practise looking and acting like men. In doing so, they bring to attention the social construction of masculinity by emphasising its visual and aural performative aspects, in this case padding their bodies to look bulky, adopting a threatening 'cocky' posture and handling heavy tools and shotguns with confidence while barking monosyllabic orders and responses in deepened voices. The sequence where the women's practice run is cut against that of Harry and his men demonstrates how the principal difference between the

5 6 7 8

women and the men is brute strength; the women find the heavy cutting equipment awkward and cumbersome to manoeuvre. In all other respects, including that of the mental work of planning and preparation, the women are shown to be equal. By foregrounding the conventions which men and women use to create acceptable images of gender difference, *Widows* exposes how gender difference is *socially* constructed – that masculinity and femininity are learnt codes of social behaviour and appearance. In order to stand a chance of winning the Miss Paddington beauty contest Shirley has to wear a range of costumes, to apply her makeup in a particular way, to practise her walking technique and rehearse the kinds of things she has to say to the judges. To earn money as an exotic dancer, Bella wears sexually provocative sado-masochistic clothing (including a metal-studded leather dog collar) and parades her body in front of the male customers she entertains. Both women have to work at producing these performances and we, as viewers, are party to the backstage work required to produce them. Whereas crime series such as *The Sweeney* treat the construction of gendered identities as an everyday aspect of creating their realist landscapes of contemporary life, 'Widows takes the construction of appearances as its central concern' (Skirrow 1985: 178).

The iconography of masculinity in Widows is not changed, merely viewed from a different perspective. Rather than straightforwardly reversing gender roles by making women the law breakers, the series is able to comment on the male-dominated police structures that shape the crime series and question women's relationship to the law and consensus morality. The women compete against three active groups of men for control of the ledgers, the money and the narrative. All their antagonists apart from Harry Rawlins see them in a one-dimensional, conventional way as subsidiary characters, people whose only value is to provide information, not generate the action or take the initiative. Unusually for the crime series, the women are not the objects of a sexual gaze; male interest in the Widows is motivated by a suspicion of their duplicity rather than by their sexual desirability. It is the women who control the look and seek to gratify their sexual desires; Lynda pursues the bisexual car mechanic Carlos, who is Arnie Fisher's boy-friend, and Dolly continues to desire Harry even though she discovers that he has a child by another (younger) woman.

In spite of these challenges to convention, the women are still dependent on men for their economic survival: Dolly and Shirley relied on their husbands; Lynda and Bella have both sold their bodies to survive. Skirrow suggests that this lack of choice in their lives may be one reason why 'they were able to break the "law" of television against successful crime and get away with it' (1985: 183), an ending that came as a surprise even to Lynda La Plante. In her original treatment La Plante abided by the unwritten rule that on television crimes must be punished and the women were caught. Executive producer Verity Lambert, undoubtedly aware that women in crime films invariably meet bad ends, said she would not produce Widows unless the women were successful and escaped with the money: 'They'd worked very hard and got it all planned – why shouldn't they get away with it'? (Alvarado and Stewart 1985: 108). Linda Agran was also firm on this point, despite La Plante's hesitancy:

> I know that some people think that the end is morally very questionable and Lynda said to me they can't get away with it, can they – the IBA wouldn't allow it. And I said, 'Nuts. Sure I'll talk to the IBA if necessary. If people are really going to get involved with it – and it is fiction – of course they're going to want them to get away with it'. (Agran in Alvarado and Stewart 1985:109)

That they do get away with it is because of yet another feminine masquerade; Shirley's mother dons a blonde wig and pretends to be Dolly, driving away from the house in Dolly's Mercedes. The men who are watching give chase, enabling Dolly and Shirley to make a run for it in Shirley's battered old Ford Fiesta.

If the father–son relationship is paradigmatic of male police partnerships in 1970s crime series, it is paralleled in *Widows* through a focus on mothers and daughters, of which the relationships between Shirley and her mother, Dolly and Shirley and Dolly and Lynda are the most notable. Shirley's mother Audrey is a hard-working, weary woman who wants her daughter to be happy; a single mother who has struggled to bring up her two children and make ends meet, she regards happiness as having enough money to live somewhere decent and pay the bills. Shirley is accustomed to being bossed about by her mother as well as helping her out financially, and easily slips into a similar role with Dolly. Lynda, abandoned by her mother as a young child, is unaccustomed to affection and actively resists Dolly's bossy concern for her. Dolly's childlessness is depicted as an aspect of her intense grief and inability to show emotion; she babies her pet dog and helps care for orphaned children in the convent.

Focusing on working-class women and their relationships was something new for the crime genre, but in many other respects *Widows* is far more conventional. Bella (Eva Mottley) is stereotypical of the kind of characters black actors had to play in the early 1980s if they wanted to work. Sarita Malik has documented how the shift in British television drama at the end of 1970s away from the literary based single play in favour of more popular genre series and serial formats had a dual effect on black representation: while 'Black people began to have an increased ongoing presence in contemporary drama on a weekly basis', this was small compensation for the fact that 'they often continued to be locked out of a whole tradition of "quality", high-budget, often heritage-based drama' (Malik 2002: 142). Black actors, faced with fewer employment opportunities, were cast in a narrower range of roles in which they were often both working class and sexualised; this had implications for representation of black people on television. In *Widows*, for example, although she is the only woman in the gang not to speak with a working-class accent, Bella is associated with drugs and prostitution, a common racial stereotype that reiterated prevalent themes in the crime series of black people as social outsiders and criminals. An obvious product of the white imagination, in the first series of *Widows* Bella exists as an isolated black character in an all-white world. Like Dolly, she first appears wearing a light grey forties-style belted mackintosh; her 'manly' appearance is commented on by a character in the amusement arcade where Lynda works. Bella is asked by Lynda to join the 'gang' in part because she *already* looks masculine; unlike Shirley, who has to work at looking and sounding like a man, Bella has a naturalised ability to act male because she lacks the conventional trappings of white femininity. White femininity, with its emphasis on codes and conventions drawn from a middle-class 'norm' that emphasises the binary oppositions between gendered identities, continues to be the cultural norm against which the characteristics of 'other' (working-class, black, lesbian) femininities are defined as 'different' (Skeggs 1997). Although *Widows* complicates conventional depictions of working-class women by presenting them as a diverse rather than a homogenous group, and as capable of doing things for themselves, arguably it does little to challenge pervasive discourses of working-class and black people as criminals and deviants other than to glamorise them. In *Widows 2*, these weaknesses become more pronounced, not least because the character of Bella is changed and she is depicted as a much more feminised character.

Widows 2

The sequel to *Widows* was broadcast two years later; although it continues the story begun in the first series, its relationship to the crime thriller is rather more conventional. Linda, Bella and Shirley are living in Rio on the proceeds of the robbery; in spite of their luxurious lifestyle, the women are restless. Dolly has returned to England to sell her house and release some money for plastic surgery while she waits to launder the rest of the stolen bank notes. Harry is in Rio looking for his share of the money and quickly finds out where Linda and Bella are living; he beats up Linda, who tells him where the money is hidden. The Widows' fear of Harry and his determination to find the money become the motors that drive the plot; although point of view remains with the women, it is Harry's desire for money and revenge that structures the narrative and motivates the Widows' (re)actions.

In interviews with Alvarado and Stewart, Lynda Agran discussed how the unexpected success of *Widows* led to pressure from Thames to make a further six episodes:

> It was very difficult because neither Lynda nor myself had any idea that we had not ended it. They've gone to Rio … Dolly just says, 'I still love him'. Finish. Now I didn't realise that people were going to get that involved with it. You know, where's Harry gone, etc.? So Thames started to make noises about doing six more to tell what happened. And I said

No, I don't want to do that. So then they said, Come on, come on, should we talk to Lynda, is she being difficult about it – doesn't she want to ... ? And I said, Look, I tell you what, I'm prepared to sit down and talk to Lynda and see if there is any chance. (Alvarado and Stewart 1985: 109)

Once Agran and La Plante sat down together to discuss it, the ideas started to flow:

and we became rather sort of caught up in it ... It's slightly worrying because I think people's expectations are raised and therefore – whereas going for *Widows* the first time was relatively easy because it was all unfamiliar – now that they've seen the first six (and I'm sure Thames will now repeat the first six and then go rocking on into the new series) this one will be more difficult. (Alvarado and Stewart 1985: 110)

The structure of the second series mirrors that of the first, only this time the suspense generated by the women committing the crime dressed as men is missing. The plot oscillates between the Widows living with the consequences of their actions, Harry and his associates, and Resnick, now a lone character with a terminal illness confined to a hospital bed. Dolly has booked a face lift and hired a private detective to take care of Harry's girlfriend and child, while Bella, having lost her opportunity to start a new life with her wealthy lover in Rio, becomes the most assertive of the younger women, vying with Dolly for control of the group. Division amongst the women results in disaster; when they meet to buy him off, Harry tries to kill Dolly. As she saves Dolly by pushing her aside, Lynda is hit by Harry's car and killed. Unbeknown to any of them (including Harry), Shirley has been recruited by Harry's accomplice to be the inside contact on Harry's latest scheme, a jewel robbery. Determined to avenge Lynda's death, Dolly and Bella eaves-drop on Harry's preparations for the raid and inform the police of his intentions. When the police bust the jewel raid, Shirley is killed in the ensuing mayhem, but Harry's accomplice escapes on a motorbike with the jewels, hotly pursued by Dolly and Bella; the bike crashes and they take the jewels. On hearing the news of Shirley's death, Dolly arranges to meet Harry to hand over the jewels; she shoots him in cold blood before the police arrive.

Filmed with an initial focus on the Widows living the high life in Rio and without the expressionist accents of the first series, the serial gestures towards the high production values of 1980s prime-time American soaps such as *Dallas* (BBC 1 1978–91) and *Dynasty* (BBC 1 1982–9).[3] Fashionable clothes, flashy jewellery and expensive cars, an exotic world of travel, luxury and far-away places create aspirational images of a celebrity lifestyle associated with pop stars, successful TV personalities and escaped criminals. The fantasy is short-lived; by the end of the second episode all the Widows are back in London and the serial lapses into a typically British form of television melodrama in the gritty, realist style that was typical of the bulk of Euston crime series. At times characters' motivations are stretched to the limits of plausibility, but these melodramatic excesses have to be viewed relative to the dominant style of television drama at the time. The 'excesses' in *Widows 2* hinge around the ways in which women's relationships with men and relationships between the women are depicted. All the women become romantically involved apart from Lynda, who remains traumatised after Harry's violent assault. Bella finds love with a rich South American, Shirley with Harry's new accomplice and Dolly's frozen emotions are thawed a little by the private detective she hires to keep track of Harry. The images of romance are typically excessive and similar to those found in popular romantic novels of the day: Bella's Latin-American lover is tall, dark and handsome as well as very rich; likewise, Harry's associate is depicted as a passionate Latin lover who seduces Shirley and literally showers her with roses. The image of Shirley lying in bed completely surrounded by bunches of dark red roses has a resonance with later 1990s melodramas such as *American Beauty* (Sam Mendes, US 1999). This romantic excess is combined with a more straight-forward, less convoluted plot structure in which the women are living with the consequences of their actions and trying to escape male violence. These themes render the women less powerful, as emotionally needy and helpless victims of their fear of Harry. The overall effect is to shift the generic ground away from the crime series towards the more conventionally 'feminine' territory of romance and melodrama.

The women's vulnerability is emphasised by a *mise-en-scène* of domestic confinement. Interiors dominate the visual landscape: Dolly's flat, the private detective's office, Resnick's hospital ward and Shirley's flat, used as the Widows' customary meeting place. Audrey, Shirley's mother, is also confined to the house because, much to Shirley's disgust, she is pregnant again. This move into domestic space fore-grounds the increasingly tense relationships between the women, shifting the generic terrain away from the streets, the public space of the crime series, towards the interior spaces of melodrama. With Harry back on the scene, the Widows become furtive. Only Shirley, the most 'feminine' of the women in conventional terms, takes control of her life; but her attempt to fulfil her ambition to become a model is ultimately her undoing and like Linda she dies, a victim of Harry's violence.

The women are not victorious this time round but there are no romantic heroes either; the shift towards melodrama is not a total one.

Throughout both series, men are depicted as unreliable and untrust-worthy, shiftless individuals who use others for money and to achieve their own aims. Far from being a 'respectable' criminal, Harry is depicted as a sadistically violent coward who deceives his own associates; his accomplice similarly deceives Shirley, while Audrey's new partner involves her son in criminal activity. Vic, the private investigator hired by Dolly, is one of the few men to seem trustworthy; he has little of the alienated, hard-boiled cynicism typical of the *noir* hero and shows growing affection for Dolly as the serial progresses. A kinder, less tormented individual than Resnick, he is neither a winner nor a loser. Resnick, on the other hand, is depicted as a police dinosaur, an extinct species consumed by obsession; the only motivation left in his empty life is to catch Harry and Dolly Rawlins. Divorced by his wife and confined to a hospital bed, his decaying body and cancerous condition embody his self-destructive fanaticism and narrative disempowerment.

Performances in *Widows 2* are also less compelling than in the first series, not least because the narrative of retribution, although well plotted, offers less opportunity to develop powerful female characters. Bella in particular, depicted as a strong, assertive character in the first series, is a very different character in the second. Eva Mottley left the series shortly after shooting for series two began, claiming sexual and racial abuse by the production crew, and was replaced by Debby Bishop (Brunsdon 1987: 191). Whereas Mottley's Bella had the anarchic, androgynous air of Grace Jones about her, Bishop's Bella is a more conventional, physically softer and less angular character who is feminised through romance with her South American lover. As a result of this change, Bella's struggle with Dolly to control the group's response to Harry appears implausible; Bishop has less screen presence than Mottley. Although she raises her voice and shouts, her body language is less self-assured. In all other respects, although Bella is no longer an isolated character, she continues to be stereotyped as a black woman. The friend she shares a flat with remains a shadowy, back-ground presence and is mistakenly beaten up instead of Bella by one of Harry's mobsters. Bella's response to Linda's questions about this, 'We all look the same in the dark, stupid', could be interpreted as sarcasm, but in tandem with the racist insults aimed at Harvey, the one black member of Harry's gang, these comments support Malik's arguments about the position of black actors within generic drama (Malik 2002). White working-class characters mouth 'plausible' racist comments in order to create a generically convincing 'realistic' image of gang relations, confirming that the only purpose of these black characters is to furnish the drama with 'authentic' background details.

In her discussion of *Widows*, Charlotte Brunsdon points out that the end of the first series prepares the way for the second by feminising Dolly, the 'strong man' of the series. The three younger women are in Rio celebrating their success; Shirley, champagne glass in hand, parodies her entry for the Miss Paddington contest, saying in a mock little-girl voice, 'I like reading, writing and robbing banks'. For Brunsdon, this moment, which 'offers parody of femininity and genre and concludes a narrative in which the women functioned as both heroes and heroines', is undercut by Dolly's subsequent entrance. Dolly reveals that Harry is still alive and that in spite of his humiliating and deceiving her, she still loves him, still desires him. The camera, accompanied by Dolly's loss theme, the lament from *Orfeo and Eurydice*, pans across the Widows' faces to finish on Dolly, shifting the generic register from crime thriller to romance. 'The move is from man's genre to women's genre, the women's genre at its most masochistic' (Brunsdon 1987: 198). The end of *Widows 2* is similarly self-punishing; with two of the Widows dead, Dolly confronts Harry as the police, tipped off by Vic, race to arrest them both. Her passion now taking the form of hatred, Dolly shoots Harry in the chest. Feminist hopes that a female producer and writer might save the female characters from their conventional narrative fates of madness, death or imprisonment are shot to pieces; Dolly is arrested, with only Bella escaping to an uncertain future abroad.

Feminist critics were not the only ones with reservations about *Widows 2*; La Plante, claiming that the second series of *Widows* (directed by Paul Annett) was 'atrociously directed', at one point withdrew her name from the production (Grant 1992: 23). Some male critics were openly disdainful, complaining of a lack of suspense in the serial and referring to the characters as the 'unsavoury in pursuit of the unlovely' (Stoddart 1985: 78). Whatever the critics thought, however, viewers tuned in and kept watching in their millions. *Widows 2* ousted Euston stable-mate *Minder* from its leading position in the ITV ratings chart and achieved audiences of more than thirteen million. By this time the series had acquired a dedicated following; Ann Mitchell and Lynda La Plante continued to receive fan mail long after it finished. They claim that Dolly's reincarnation some ten years later in *She's Out* came about because a fan reminded them that Dolly was due to be released. In the intervening years La Plante pursued other projects, but she had to wait until 1990 before her third drama, *Prime Suspect*, was accepted for television.

Strong women and feminist criticism

One of the critical issues to emerge from these early years of female-authored drama is whether the gender of the writer actually did make a difference to the representations of women on the screen. The short answer is, of course, yes, undoubtedly it did; for the first time women appeared in leading roles in a masculine genre such as the crime thriller in their own right, not as wives and girlfriends of leading men or subject to male authority. *Widows* was not only written by a woman but also produced by women, proving that women could make series and serials that were popular and commercially successful as well as exciting and different, offering something new. Why then were feminist critics so constrained in their response to La Plante's work? Part of the problem lay in the nature of the feminist critical project and its strong links to literary and film studies. Popular television drama presented problems that traditional academic approaches to cultural texts were unable to resolve, not least because of the popular and commercial nature of the texts themselves. Unlike a film or play, television texts tend to be fragmented and segmented, the flexi-narrative structure of their series and serial formats intercut not only with other plot strands but with advertisements, announcements and news casts. Their low status as 'texts' has tended to focus critical attention on issues of representation and reception, with only the work of a few (male) television dramatists given conventional critical attention. This critical impasse remains something of a problem for those traditionally denied authorship status, a situation further complicated by the spectre of essentialism that any exploration of female authorship as 'women's writing' quickly raises. Nonetheless, some exploration of why La Plante's texts were not wholeheartedly received by those who had championed the cause of the woman writer and the greater visibility of women in popular television is undoubtedly warranted.

There was in 1970s feminism a streak of essentialism that believed values coded as 'feminine' in western culture, such as mutual co-operation, emotional responsibility and lack of individual ambition, were superior to values coded as 'masculine' such as individual ambition, aggression and competition. This created a suspicion of representations of 'strong' women, women who seemed to adopt 'masculine' behaviours and attitudes in pursuit of their own ambitions. Factors at work in the broader social and political landscape of the 1980s tended to confirm fears that 'strong' women were not only 'masculine' in their social behaviours and attitudes; they were associated with radical right-wing politics, the British Conservative party and its leader Prime Minister

Margaret Thatcher. For the first time women were becoming more visible on the world stage, with important consequences for mediating women's experiences. The sign 'woman' drifted away from its 1970s 'earthmother' image towards a more authoritarian matriarchal representation embodied in Thatcher's popular construction as the 'iron lady' of British politics, while at the same time encompassing a more self-assertive 'girlie' sexuality personified by the North American pop star Madonna. There was of course nothing new in these images of themselves; authoritarian matriarchs and glamorous 'naughty' seductresses are constitutive of the virgin–whore dichotomy that has underpinned images of women in western patriarchal culture since ancient times. What was of interest to feminist cultural critics were the ways in which these two contrasting images of women were differently appropriated by the media to represent the 'new woman' of the 1980s and present the case that the battle for equal rights had been won. In what was regarded at the time as a feminist backlash (a seductive thesis to some feminists because it seems to offer an explanation of feminism's failure), numerous commentators argued that with a queen on the throne, a woman running the government and Madonna at the top of the hit parade, women in the UK were entering a 'post-feminist' era of equality and openness between the sexes; the battle for female emancipation was over and women had very little to complain about (Faludi 1992).

The election of Margaret Thatcher as prime minister in 1979 began more than a decade of Conservative government that changed Britain irrevocably. Voted in on the strength of promises to increase personal wealth, reduce public spending, dismantle the welfare state and privatise Britain's nationalised industries, Thatcher put forward neo-liberal economic policies and right-wing views on contentious issues such as law and order, immigration and defence that were a source of concern for feminists, many of whom were allied to a socialist/left-wing Labour agenda orientated towards redistributing wealth rather than concentrating it in fewer and fewer hands. Thatcher's radical agenda depended upon her ability to win widespread support for change; associating social democracy with an overly bureaucratic state and outdated systems of social welfare, she mobilised popular ideology, aligning herself with 'the people'. Stuart Hall (1988) labelled Thatcher's strategies 'authoritarian populism'; issues of rising crime, juvenile delinquency and immigration articulated through discourses of popular morality were invoked to play on the fears and anxieties of ordinary people. Famously declaring that there is no such thing as society, Thatcher advocated a return to nineteenth-century middle-class family values of thrift, self-reliance and personal responsibility. A key metaphor used by Thatcher was to compare the running of the nation's economy to the balancing of the household budget; in a similar way to the good housewife who shops around to find the best-value food to feed her family, so government officials and the public servants of the 'nanny' state have a duty and a responsibility to shop around and provide the best-value services for their 'customers'.

The handbag and the shopping bag became symbols of a decade during which the number of people in poverty increased from five million in 1979 (9 per cent) to over fourteen million; publicly owned utilities such as electricity, gas and water were sold into private ownership and heavy industries such as steel manufacturing and coal mining were denationalised. The decline of manufacturing industries, particularly in the north, and the rise of the service sector accentuated north–south divisions; by the end of the 1980s Liverpool, for example, was the poorest city in Europe. During the decade, the nation became far wealthier (the incomes of the wealthiest 10 per cent of the population increased by over 60 per cent between 1979 and 1992), but that wealth was concentrated in the hands of fewer people. Beggars appeared on British streets in significant numbers as unemployment doubled between 1979 and 1982, remaining at more than three million until 1986, the highest figure since the 1930s. These changes had significant gender implications; more women were working than ever before, most of them in part-time, low-paid service-sector jobs. The same disparity was shared by minority groups – amongst young British Afro-Caribbean men between eighteen and nineteen, the unemployment rate rose to over 43 per cent.

In contrast to the image of the authoritarian matriarch embodied in Margaret Thatcher and her policies, the pop star Madonna offered young women (and men) an image of active female sexuality centred around what columnist Suzanne Moore called the 'insatiable clitoris' (Andermahr 1994: 29). Rising to prominence in the mid-1980s, Madonna quickly developed a reputation for her playful appropriations of gender and sexuality in songs and videos such as 'Like a Virgin' and 'Justify my Love'. Her auto-erotic, self-pleasuring simulated sexual activity with men and women brought gay subculture centre stage, disturbing the virgin–whore dichotomy by playing with what feminist critic Camille Paglia celebrated as 'the dazzling profusion of her mercurial sexual personae' and her knowing games with the 'animality and the artifice [of sex]' (Andermahr 1994: 30). Whether recreating the screen icons of the past, such as the cross-dressing Marlene Dietrich and highly sexualised Marilyn Monroe, or posing in her infamously

phallic Jean-Paul Gaultier cone-shaped bra with its bisexual connota-
tions, Madonna raided the visual language of sexual difference, playing
with, parodying and parading femininity in performances that
encapsulated the essence of 'camp'. Gay icon and mainstream star,
Madonna brought the margins to the centre, her (re)presentation of
sexuality as performance and femininity as a mask revealing the social
construction of gendered identities in western culture (Andermahr
1994: 33). For critics interested in studying issues of representation and
identity, Madonna's humorous self-parody and aggressive displays of
female desire fuelled post-modern debates about the provisional and
fragmented nature of all identities; for others, her spectacular constructions of sexual difference perpetuated objectification of women by
presenting the gendered image as a commodity, an image for sale.

Unlike other twentieth-century icons, however, Madonna retained
full financial and managerial control of the production, marketing and
distribution of her image(s) and songs. She was, in the words of one of
her own songs, the quintessential 'material girl', beating the boys at
their own game. In this sense she represents a shift in regimes of
representation not only at the level of appearances but also in terms of
ownership of the means of production; her business skills and financial
acumen demonstrated that women could control their creative and
financial destinies by becoming capitalists in their own right. The
increasing economic power of some women, a result in part of widen-
ing opportunities in the workplace for educated middle-class women,
contributed to a decade in which conspicuous consumption of goods
and services, images and identities grew apace irrespective of earnings.
Personal image and 'lifestyle' were marketed as keys to individual
success; magazines such as *Company* and *Cosmopolitan* were at the
forefront of projecting images of the 'new woman', establishing a niche
market around the lifestyle of the 'working girl', a young, single city
office worker and emergent professional woman (Lee 1988: 166–73).
Married women were bombarded by images of successful 'superwomen'
such as Shirley Conran and Anita Roddick, high-flying achievers
projected by the media as successful jugglers who could meet the
conflicting demands of work and business, home and family life,
constructing a glamorous persona of 'women on top' that exuded wealth
as the key to personal fulfilment. During the 1980s Thatcher herself
underwent a series of physical 'makeovers' designed to make her appear
more glamorous and more feminine, changing the colour and style of
her hair, makeup and wardrobe, altering her teeth and training her
voice to remove all trace of its more strident tones.

While some feminists saw the harnessing of consumer discourses to feminism as the co-option of feminism's radical potential and as a means of 'inoculating' women against militant actions such as the anti-Cruise missile campaign mounted at Greenham Common,[4] others viewed these new discourses as significant shifts in regimes of representation and formations of social identity that opened up new sites of struggle. In part, this was a generational split; 1970s feminism was very different in tone and character from what is often termed 'post-feminism', the decades following the 1970s when feminism became far more divided and differentiated, deconstructing many of the precepts of the 1970s. Without wanting to make more than the broadest of generalisations, there is a sense amongst many historians of feminism that the 1970s were characterised by a more puritanical, anti-consumer ethos than the decades that followed. Brunsdon (1993) argues that the most common position in feminist criticism at this time was a 'recruitist' one, the impulse to transform feminine identifications of women into feminist ones. In the 1970s many feminist activists and critics wanted to see media images of 'liberated' women, women freed from the conventional signifying systems that contained and defined them as stereotypes *only* in relation to men (as mothers, wives, daughters, girlfriends, nurses, secretaries, prostitutes, etc.). Although these stereotypes were found across all forms of popular culture – in magazines, advertising, films and romantic novels – representations of women on television were regarded as especially invidious because of television's claim on reality, particularly in its live form. Unlike other media such as films or newspapers, television's unique status is in part defined by its ability to transmit live the sounds and images of events as they are happening; in this sense, the camera's status as a witness to events added veracity to its claims to tell the truth, to be a 'window on the world'. John Caughie has argued that one of the fascinations that early television offered its viewers was the sense of things happening now, 'before visual language had a chance to impose order', an experience he terms 'the rush of the real' (2000a: 100). Perhaps this was a spectre that haunted feminist critics' and activists' perceptions of how 'other' women who were not feminists (and therefore, by definition, not aware of the underlying power structure between women and men in a male-dominated society) were kept in a state of 'false consciousness', seduced by the apparent 'reality' of the paternalistic world on their television screens.

Feminist critics therefore sought texts that would support them in their project of creating different horizons of expectation for all women. With so few programmes or dramas produced or written by women in the early stages of television, and with most of what was written constrained by the professional practices of male producers, directors and technical crews, the notion of what a feminist programme or drama on television might or could look and sound like was at best an imaginary one, constructed from other discourses about female-authored texts in other media, primarily in the case of television drama *avant-garde* film. In many ways this was an association dictated by the nature of the media (both film and television produce moving images with sound) rather than by the context in which such forms and practices could and did evolve. Independent film and video practice developed within the context of Arts Council and British Film Institute subsidised funding structures; feminist aesthetics in *avant-garde* films of the late 1970s and early 1980s are marked by anti-narrative structures and anti-realist styles. Many of the films aim to critique and deconstruct the regimes and mechanisms of representation used in the mainstream by engaging with the formal processes of signification itself. Feminist filmmaking practice advocated the deconstruction of conventional narrative paradigms, the stripping away of familiar and recognisable associations, the making strange of the viewing experience in the interests of forging new meanings around the over-determined sign 'woman' and privileging a 'feminine voice'; notable examples of such films include *Daughter Rite* (Citron 1978), *Riddles of the Sphinx* (Mulvey 1979) and *Thriller* (Potter 1979) (Kuhn 1982; Brunsdon 1986).

The elite arts-based practices and discourses of independent film and video production were, however, an inappropriate model to use to evaluate female authorship in the commercially dominated and ratings-orientated world of television drama – not least because the one space potentially open to the kinds of experimentation and innovation favoured by many feminist and left-wing critics, the single play, was unavailable to women. As Madelaine Macmurraugh-Kavanagh has convincingly argued, female writers were effectively squeezed out of the single-play slot at the very moment that feminist ideas were gaining ground in the UK. Confined to writing popular series and serial drama, female scriptwriters, unlike their male counterparts, had no access to a televisual space where they could develop their work unhindered by the requirement of having to address a mass audience. This left the question of how to talk about women's writing for television in something of a vacuum; the writers who had achieved a measure of success were working in popular genres such as comedy (Carla Lane) and the crime thriller (La Plante), genres considered to be formulaic, conventional and conformist, if not blatantly reactionary.

The feminist critical response to such works, perhaps most clearly articulated in the UK context by Charlotte Brunsdon (1987), was to use them as sites to think through the relationship between gender and genre, between television and its audiences. The gender of the writer and producer of a series or serial was of much less interest than the questions of form and problems of representation that arise 'in the attempt to produce different, popular, pleasurable and recognisable representations of women' (Brunsdon 1997: 68). Because the work of women scriptwriters and dramatists was often considered conventional and unchallenging by feminist critics, it was ignored or critically condemned. Looking back at *Widows* some twenty years later, it becomes clear that the changes wrought by La Plante in the structure of the crime series and its representations of women were to have a lasting impact on the genre. However, it took a further groundbreaking drama from La Plante to decisively shift the UK crime genre away from its preoccupation with action series into the psychological territory of the thriller more commonly associated with contemporary variants of the form. As well as offering further challenges to those seeking different, pleasurable and popular representations of women, La Plante's next successful series, *Prime Suspect*, shot both author and star to the top of the UK ratings and confirmed La Plante's status as Britain's most innovative and controversial writer of popular television drama.

Notes

1 Thames lost its franchise following changes in criteria introduced by the Tory government in 1989; its back catalogue at time of writing is owned by Pearson/ Freemantle Media.
2 Mitchell was awarded the Pye Award for 'Female Who Had the Greatest Impact on TV' in 1983. The entire cast of *Widows* won a 'TV Personality of the Year' award.
3 For a discussion of the melodramatic aspect of these soaps, see Feuer 1995: 111–30.
4 The women's peace camp around the American airbase at Greenham Common near Newbury, Berkshire lasted from 1981 to 2000; women from all walks of life took part in a sustained campaign to remove the US nuclear Cruise missile bases from British soil, some living for many months and years at the camps around the base. When the missiles were removed in 1989, the peace camp continued as a protest against nuclear war.

Gender, genre, star

3

In the same year that Assistant Police Constable for Merseyside Alison Halford decided to take her employers to court for sexual discrimination in the workplace, La Plante successfully sold her third crime series to Granada Television. Starring Helen Mirren as Detective Chief Inspector Jane Tennison, a career-orientated policewoman determined to reach the top of her profession, *Prime Suspect* was an immediate success. Shown on consecutive evenings in April 1991, the two-part four-hour mini-series was watched by more than fourteen million viewers; it was repeated with similar success the following December on Channel 4.

The *Prime Suspect* series is La Plante's most successful to date, winning numerous international awards for Lynda La Plante herself, the producers Granada and Helen Mirren. *Prime Suspect 2* and *Prime Suspect 3* followed, the second series written by Alan Cubitt based on a storyline by La Plante, the third written by La Plante herself. At this point, La Plante severed her connection with the series; three further productions starring Helen Mirren have been developed by Granada using different writers. The fifth series, *Prime Suspect: Errors of Judgement*, shown in Britain in 1996, was broadcast in seventy-eight countries around the world. Between them, the show and its star have received more than fourteen international awards, including several BAFTAs for best series and best actor, three Prime-time Emmy awards for best mini-series and a Special Emmy for outstanding lead actress in a mini-series. On completion of *Prime Suspect 5*, Mirren declared that she was leaving the series because she did not want to become typecast or overassociated with the role of DCI Tennison, effectively eliminating the character and the series that she had made very much her own. This was not quite the end of the story however; in July 2003, after a gap of seven years, she was back on the set for a new series broadcast the following November. *Prime Suspect 6*, written by Peter Berry, has again won awards for its writer and star.[1]

In this chapter, the focus is on the first three series that La Plante created and wrote and the contexts, industrial, cultural and critical, in which they were produced and received. In the first *Prime Suspect* (1991), Tennison is determined to advance her career by taking over a murder case, a job reserved for the boys in obvious breach of non-discriminatory employment practices. She has to overcome the misogynistic working practices of the Metropolitan Police Force and prove herself to the all-male hierarchy by successfully arresting a suspected serial killer and bringing him to trial. In *Prime Suspect 2* (1992) Tennison is seeking promotion when a high-profile and politically sensitive investigation of the murder of a young black woman reveals the institutional racism ingrained in police culture and practices; she has to confront her own prejudices as well as those of her fellow officers in order to solve the crime. In *Prime Suspect 3* (1993), themes of sexual exploitation and murder continue alongside revelations of paedophilia and homophobia in an episode initially written by Lynda La Plante but changed in several places by the producers. Unhappy with the lack of control she could exert in developing her ideas, with being treated as 'just a writer for hire' (Lawson 1998: 86), La Plante left the series at the end of this production to start her own company.

Between writing the first series of *Widows* and developing *Prime Suspect*, La Plante was caught up in the whirlwind of change in broadcasting as technological and economic imperatives transformed the ways in which the industry was organised internally, affecting the ways in which drama was commissioned and produced. The opening in 1982 of the second commercial channel, Channel 4, with its brief to serve minority interests and represent people without a voice on the other three channels, can in retrospect be seen as the last gasp of a public broadcasting system struggling to maintain outdated notions of 'quality' and value amidst contending financial pressures and demographic change. The 1980s saw the introduction in the UK of VHS video recorders as 'must have' household items, with ownership figures among the highest in the western hemisphere. For the first time viewers had more control over what they watched, time-shifting and self-scheduling their viewing. With the introduction of cable and satellite broadcasting multi-channel viewing became a reality for some subscribers as Rupert Murdoch's Sky and the British-owned consortium British Satellite Broadcasting (BSB) prepared to do battle for the viewers' fingers on their remote control buttons (Crisell 1997).

With new technology making more choices available to viewers, the ways in which television was used and viewed changed inexorably; as the age of cable and satellite broadcasting dawned slowly over the suburban heartlands, terrestrial broadcasters became ever more competitive in their fight for ratings. The BBC, under increasing pressure from the Conservative government to justify funding from a licence fee, had to prove it could still provide quality and value for money. Director-General Michael Checkland, significantly the first director-general who was an accountant not a programme maker, streamlined the internal management structures to make departments more cost effective. Under the new regime, drama departments lost their autonomy to commissioning editors, the only people with the power to greenlight projects (Goodwin 1998: 125–32). The new managerial ethos aimed to create internal competition; initially it created internal chaos as the institutional culture of the BBC was changed from the top down. Hence writers such as La Plante found themselves in the position where projects initially instigated by keen producers sat on people's desks waiting for commissioners to decide whether they should be made.

The ITV network also suffered the ravages of change as the first generation of owners and managers reached retiring age. Changes in the composition of the ITV network followed in the wake of the Broadcasting Act of 1990, which altered the way in which broadcast franchises were allocated to companies by introducing a new process of regulated tendering that included a high 'quality' threshold. Thames Television lost its licence to Carlton in the bidding process, leading some commentators to suspect that the Conservative government had made a deliberate move to punish Thames for not supporting them on crucial political issues – although such claims remained unproven (Goodwin 1998: 115–16). Those who were successful in gaining a franchise faced increased competition for advertising revenue; for some companies, the high tariff they paid for their broadcast franchise created a leaner financial environment in which efficiency and economies of scale were essential for financial survival. The Broadcasting Act demanded that there should be 'fair competition' in the supply of programmes to the ITV network; all broadcasters were charged with diversifying their output by commissioning 25 per cent of their product from independent production companies. Most broadcast companies saw this as an opportunity to downsize their production staff and streamline their in-house production methods, creating a shift in the way that programmes were commissioned and made that had particular implications for Lynda La Plante's development as a writer and as a producer of her own work, discussed in more detail in Chapter 4.

Importing popular prime-time American series was one way in which terrestrial broadcasters, constantly aware of their ratings, attempted to hold on to prime time audiences. On ITV in particular, the female viewer's tastes were increasingly catered for; BBC audience research in 1984 noted that the demographic of the ITV audience tended towards older working-class and semi-professional or lower-middle-class women (Hallam 2005). Popular television drama, particularly programmes imported from America, engaged with changing images of feminine authority and female desire through their leading female characters. If Dolly Rawlins in *Widows* had a matriarchal authoritarian streak and a professionalism that matched the determination of Margaret Thatcher (but not her class background), Joan Collins's portrayal of Alexis Carrington/Colby/Dexter in the US import *Dynasty* embraced the successful businesswoman and the adulterous wife, the loving mother and the spiderwoman, her glamorous older-woman persona a potent image of mature feminine sexuality and female economic power. With other images of 'strong' women in US series such as the New York cops Christine Cagney and Mary-Beth Lacey shifting the representation of women on the small screen towards more assertive forms of feminine behaviour, albeit through a focus on their personal relationships rather than their professional lives, writers and producers of popular drama in Britain began to be a little more adventurous.

As noted in the last chapter, equal opportunities legislation had made some inroads into sexual discrimination in the workplace; there were more female writers, more female producers and many more women appearing in dramas in leading roles by the mid-1980s. Consequently, the range of representations on the screen began to broaden, with women appearing more frequently in professional roles, albeit that many of these were couched in terms of a liberal equal opportunities agenda that worked against radical feminists' efforts to create programmes with a distinctive feminist outlook (Baehr and Dyer 1987: 117–30). In this more competitive environment, broadcasters realised that the diverse tastes of the viewing public (albeit addressed in terms of 'lifestyle' groups) had to be catered for as well as the demands of advertisers seeking 'lifestyle' niche markets. The female audience could no longer be considered a 'lumpen proletariat' mass; their preferences began to dictate not only the early evening schedule but prime time too. By the end of the decade, popular contemporary dramas written and/or produced by women and starring women, such as *South of the Border* (BBC 1 1988), *Making Out* (BBC 1 1989–91) and *The Manageress* (C4 1989–90), had extended the range of roles available to women beyond the early evening soaps into prime-time drama.

La Plante has often spoken about how after the success of *Widows* and *Widows 2* she found it difficult to get new projects commissioned; most executive producers and drama controllers wanted more of the same kind of characters and storyline. By this time she was working on other ideas, including the treatment that would become *Civvies*, but with the project shelved by the BBC she turned her hand to writing novels, producing *The Legacy* (1987), *The Talisman* (1989), *Bella Mafia* (1990) and *Entwined* (1992) all of which sold moderately well. Talking to Sean Day-Lewis, La Plante describes how *Prime Suspect* evolved:

> By the time I went to see Granada that time I was desperate ... the script editor Jenny Sheridan said, 'We are looking for big dramas'. So I said, 'Oh good, I've got one'. 'We really want another police show', she said. 'As it happens I've got one', I repeated. I had absolutely nothing really and was trying to feel 'What do they want?' I said. 'She's a policewoman and very tough'. She asked for a title and I said *Prime Suspect* just like that. She said they were very interested and would I send the treatment. (Day-Lewis 1998: 85)

La Plante's next step was to ring the Metropolitan Police and ask to meet high-ranking officers who were not in uniform. Their response was to say that they had numerous senior women she could talk to, but in fact there were only four. She was introduced to Detective Chief Inspector Jackie Malton and became her shadow for six months. La Plante describes Malton as an extraordinary woman who took her to forensic and pathology and thoroughly acquainted her with the day-to-day detail of police procedure. As well as providing a template for the character who became Jane Tennison, Malton has remained an advisor to La Plante, checking all her police scripts for accuracy. Subsequently Malton ran her own company advising film and television makers on various aspects of police procedure and police life.

In spite of their initial enthusiasm, Granada declined La Plante's script when she submitted it because a number of people thought the character might be too strong for mass-audience tastes; it was sent to the ITV drama pool to be considered by other commercial broadcasters. A number of them showed interest in bidding for the series, refuelling Granada's interest with the result that executive producer Sally Head decided to put the drama into production. Script editor Jenny Sheridan's belief in the project helped steer it through the production process thereafter, ensuring that much of the controversial content was not edited out (Day-Lewis 1998: 85).[2]

Significantly for La Plante's development as a writer, prime-time television drama in Britain at this time was becoming increasingly 'star' led, with implications for the kinds of subject matter that could be tackled as well as the way in which writers could treat it. In an interview with Mark Lawson for *Front Row*, Howard Brenton, a veteran of the 'golden age' of the single play and responsible for five episodes of the BBC's second series of the spy thriller *Spooks* (BBC 2003), describes this shift as one from writing about anti-heroes to a focus on heroes but claims it is still possible for drama to air contemporary fears and anxieties (BBC Radio 4, 10 June 2003).

The pressure on writers of TV drama at this particular time was to write mini-series – perhaps because, as Glen Creeber suggests, the use of cumulative multi-narrative storylines encourages audience involvement and 'more successfully exploits the fundamental dynamics of television consumption', holding on to viewers from one night to the next (Creeber 2001b: 36). Rather than waiting until the following week and risking viewer 'forgetfulness', the four-hour mini-series shown on consecutive evenings keeps viewers firmly engaged. The increasing popularity of mini-series with drama commissioners had consequences for critically prestigious single-play anthology series such as *Play for Today* (BBC 1970–84) and *Play of the Month* (BBC 1965–79, 1982–3), which were squeezed from the schedules in favour of what some critics regarded as the 'bastard hybrid' of the made-for-TV movie scheduled with similar portmanteau titles such as *Film on Four* and *Screen Two* (Auty 1985, Caughie 1991, Ansorge 1997). Some writers regarded the end of the single play as the end of an era of experimentalism and innovation in which individuals could produce socially and politically 'progressive' drama; Alan Plater, for example, regards the internal cost-accounting measures introduced at the BBC and the restraints placed upon regional drama production as anathema to the creation of a broad spectrum of work where young and new writers had 'a place to learn the trade in gentle stages, without metropolitan controllers breathing down the producer's neck' (Plater 2000: 71). If, for some, it was the end of a 'golden age' of patronage, for others the changes offered new opportunities. Memorable dramas produced in the early 1990s include lesbian coming-of-age drama *Oranges Are Not the Only Fruit* (BBC 2 1990) by Jeanette Winterson (her own adaptation of her award-winning novel), Lucy Gannon's stories of military wives and their husbands *Soldier, Soldier* (ITV 1991–6), Meera Syal's play *My Sister-Wife* (BBC 2 1992) and Hanif Kureishi's adaptation of his novel of British Asian life in the 1970s *The Buddha of Suburbia* (BBC 1 1993).[3]

The split between authorial works and popular genre products that characterises approaches and attitudes to British television drama at this time was dramatically demonstrated at the BAFTA awards of 1992, in events dubbed in the press of the day the 'Baftagate' affair.[4]

Accusations of rigged voting followed the narrow defeat of Alan Bleasdale's *GBH* (C4 1991) for the coveted writer's award which was presented to Lynda La Plante for *Prime Suspect*.[5] Pitched against each other as potential winners of the prestigious award, the two Merseyside writers represented very different traditions of writing drama – one of which was arguably in decline, the other in the ascendance. *GBH* was a thinly veiled analogy of events in Liverpool during the mid-1980s when the city council was controlled by the left-wing Militant Tendency. Serialised as a seven-episode ten-hour polemical drama for Channel 4, the ambitious script epitomised the authorial status of the writer as a 'speaker of opinions' concerning the social and political events that catapulted the city into open conflict with the Tory government.[6] For many critics, Bleasdale's serial continued to articulate the values of the single play at its most critical and socially analytical in the more extended contemporary format of the serial.

With the security of their 'tenure' rapidly eroded by a changing system of values, authors and producers who had benefited from the patronage afforded by public-service values were understandably concerned by 'Baftagate'. The following year Dennis Potter, regarded as the quintessential television dramatist and a living embodiment of the authorial ideals and values espoused by liberal humanist critics, spoke out publicly in defence of the single play in a guest lecture at the Edinburgh International Television Festival. Potter had developed from a writer of single plays in the 1960s and 1970s to a writer of mini-series and serials in the 1980s – of which *The Singing Detective* (BBC 1986) is regarded by many critics as one of the finest realisations of the novelistic potential of television drama (see, for example, Caughie 2000a, Cook 1995, Creeber 1998, W. Stephen Gilbert 1997). Potter's body of work secured his position at the apex of the male-dominated hierarchy of 'quality' drama, a position he retained until his death in 1994 in spite of the relative failure of later productions such as the self-directed *Blackeyes* (BBC 2 1989) – described by some critics as a near pornographic fantasy – and *Lipstick on Your Collar* (C4 1993), which relied on what became a Potter trademark, lip-synching actors to popular songs of the day. Potter took advantage of his position behind the lectern to lambaste Director-General John Birt and Chairman Marmaduke Hussey for introducing the internal market into the BBC in what became a high-profile defence of the values of public-service broadcasting and the patronage it had afforded a certain kind of writing (Potter 1993). This patronage was however highly selective in terms of both the themes and the forms of drama it favoured, as subsequent research by Macmurraugh-Kavanagh has shown.

It is in this sense that Lynda La Plante's victory at the BAFTA awards represented a shift at the heart of the British television establishment in terms of evaluating drama. By selecting a writer of popular genre series, the Academy acknowledged that genre writing was not of itself a barrier to excellence: formal and stylistic limitations could provide a stimulus for creative and innovative work that challenges the status quo in both generic and wider institutional terms while meeting the commercial demands of the marketplace (for a development of this argument see Macmurraugh-Kavanagh 2000a: 40–9). In terms of the wider debate about 'quality' drama, however, La Plante's victory was viewed as a 'feminisation' of the 'masculine' values of objectivity and restraint associated with the single play, a retreat from the values of public-service broadcasting and its standards in favour of the ethos of the marketplace. In the increasingly commercial environment of British television, she was regarded by some as exploiting the broadcasters' equal opportunities agenda for commissioning dramas written by writers from non-mainstream groups that featured marginalised subjects in key roles, and her work received little by way of serious critical attention (Hallam 2000b). Whatever the critical view, one thing was certain: La Plante had smashed her way through the glass ceiling in UK television drama to become the UK's top writer in what was traditionally regarded as a 'men only' genre.

Sexual textual politics: (re)writing the crime series

> Jane Tennison is someone who absolutely and uncompromisingly doesn't do anything that you could call feminine. She is a character who has rejected manipulation which, historically, is the way that women have gained power. (Helen Mirren in Miller, 1996: 96)

The female detective has a long history in popular crime fiction, her emergence on television occurring relatively late in the day. Eight years before the publication of John Stuart Mill's acclaimed emancipatory text *The Subjection of Women* (1869) an imaginary female sleuth was escaping from a dull life of genteel poverty by going about her business at Scotland Yard. In the US the first woman to write detective fiction was Anna Katherine Green (1846–1935), who created the forerunner of one of the most well-known types, the 'elderly busybody' detective embodied in Agatha Christie's 1930s creation Miss Marple. Throughout the twentieth century, female sleuths of all ages and types appeared in various guises (as nurses, secretaries, wives and elderly spinsters as well as detectives and private investigators) in popular girls' magazines, periodicals and paperback novels, many of them created by female authors (Craig and Cadogan 1981: 11). In spite of their widespread popularity, surprisingly few of these enterprising women have found their way onto UK and US film and television screens apart from Christie's Miss Marple, played numerous times by various leading actresses, each of whom has brought her own particular interpretation to the role (Jansson 1998).

The American hard-boiled tradition of detective writing was rewritten in the 1970s and 1980s by liberal feminist authors such as Sara Paretsky, Marcia Muller, Linda Barnes, Lisa Cody and Sue Grafton, all of whom take the model of the cynical, world weary private eye and reimagine him as a woman. It is perhaps unsurprising that in a decade marked by the right-wing policies of the Thatcher and Reagan administrations, the independent female sleuth, usually in the form of the private detective, offered unrivalled opportunity for authorial commentary on gender and racial exploitation, corporate corruption and murder (Munt 1994; Walton and Jones 1999). These writers subvert the traditionally 'masculine' form of the crime thriller by investigating the misogyny and corruption that lie at the (hard) core of the genre's structure. Although highly popular, the books were largely ignored by the American film industry; only Paretsky's work has been adapted, combining the plots of two of her novels into a film version that stars Kathleen Turner as the eponymous hero V.I. Warshawski. Hollywood tends to favour female investigators who become victims, such as Clarice Starling (Jodie Foster) in *Silence of the Lambs* (Demme 1991) and Sigourney Weaver and Holly Hunter in *Copycat* (Amiel 1995), rather than enterprising, intelligent and successful women, or a focus on women whose sexuality is the subject of (male) investigation, a common feature of new *film noir* (sometimes termed *neo-noir*) and a regular staple of Hollywood movies since the 1970s (Tasker 1998).

Television has offered greater opportunities for the female investigator, albeit usually inscribed and constrained within the framework of law and order institutions and genre texts.[7] Notable amongst police procedural series was the feminist-inspired US drama *Cagney and Lacey* (CBS 1982–8) conceived by Barbara Avedon and Barbara Corday. Despite high audience ratings and winning a number of Emmy awards, the series was eventually cancelled because it invoked problematic definitions of female sexuality, particularly in relation to Christine Cagney, an independent unmarried woman who has an intense relationship with her female working partner Mary Beth (D'Acci 1994). Although women had appeared as detectives in prime-time US series such as *Policewoman* and *Charlie's Angels*, as well as being skilled working women these characters were depicted as glamorous sex objects subject to male authority. *Cagney and Lacey* shifted the genre away from action and glamour, favouring realism and a focus on the women's personal lives. In the first series Cagney and Lacey are depicted as tougher and rougher than earlier female police characters, an aspect of their position as working-class urban women who have to work for economic reasons. Because these working-class characters stray away from the safe middle (-class) ground of 'respectable' femininity *Cagney and Lacey* created problems for its producers, opening space for debate and contestation of the characters' sexual identities. Three increasingly feminine, glamorous actresses played the Cagney role in an attempt to rein in the character and quell the charges of lesbianism that the female 'buddy' role incited, but none succeeded in constraining the character within traditional conceptions of heterosexual femininity. The replacement of Loretta Swit with Meg Foster, and then of Foster with Sharon Gless had mixed results for the programme makers. Although the 'new' Cagney as played by Gless was softer and more glamorous in her appearance than Foster's, the character continued to exhibit 'unfeminine' behavioural characteristics such as aggression, impatience and heavy drinking. As one perceptive critic noted at the time, Cagney and Lacey are human beings, not just women; whenever women start acting like human beings, they are accused of trying to be men (D'Acci 1994: 112).

In her definitive study of the production and reception of the series, Julie D'Acci points out how vested institutional, political, cultural and 'personal' interests in definitions of woman, women and femininity were played out in much of the commentary generated by the show. In this struggle for meaning Cagney and Lacey were frequently cited as 'real' women in relation to pervasive TV representations of 'stereotypical' women, a positioning that hinged on definitions of their bodies as territories to be fought for.

On British television in the early 1990s, *Prime Suspect* is arguably a similar site of struggle, albeit on a smaller scale, with a range of discursive formations mobilised to delimit and 'naturalise' the provocative figure of DCI Jane Tennison, as discussed in more detail below. Tennison ventured where other female detectives on television had feared to tread, her penetrating gaze unveiling the corrupt and misogynistic practices of the Masonic brotherhood that controlled UK policing, an investigation given enhanced plausibility by the high-profile court case surrounding the Assistant Chief Constable of Merseyside Police, Alison Halford. Halford took her employers to an industrial tribunal using the powers granted to her by equal opportunities legislation after she was refused promotion to Chief Constable for the ninth time. During the highly publicised events that followed, stories of Halford's partying and inappropriate entertaining were passed to the press; she was accused of entertaining other officers in poolside parties, with strong implications of nudity and inappropriate sexual behaviour. Halford resigned from the police in an out-of-court settlement, her case and the publicity surrounding it undoubtedly enhancing *Prime Supect*'s claims to authenticity. Although Lynda La Plante denies any direct connection between Tennison's ambitions and Halford's experiences, there is no doubt that she intended the depiction of an ambitious woman banging her head against the glass ceiling to strike a chord with the prime-time female audience.

The first *Prime Suspect* was hailed by the press as a gritty text, one that created new standards of realism in the genre. When questioned about her style of writing, La Plante is usually evasive, maintaining that everything she writes is true, based on extensive personal research and observation of her characters. Like the investigative detective she created, she is obsessive about the accuracy of the details, locating herself in a tradition of realism (sometimes termed naturalism) that is centred on the primacy of the author as a witness, a meticulous recorder of what she or he sees.[8] The conditions of work and the procedural practices represented in *Prime Suspect* are undoubtedly accurate and based on La Plante's thorough research as Jackie Malton's shadow, accompanying her to post mortems, observing forensic procedures and noting the ways in which Malton had to constantly negotiate the all-male environment that she worked in from day to day. In contrast to La Plante's intentions to map in detail the social reality that she perceives (echoing the detailed expositional descriptions of nineteenth-century naturalists) her crime dramas in performance are heavily stylised, evoking the oppressive, corrupt atmosphere characteristic of new *film noir* as well as realism and its ever-present partner in television genre texts, melodrama. The combination of these three elements, all evoking a familiar range of televisual and filmic codes and conventions, create in the *Prime Suspect* series a multi-layering of narrative and affect where meaning is always in process, mobilised through reference to other crime texts and popular genres as well as through external associations such as the press reporting of the Halford case and personal knowledge and experience of policing and law-and-order issues. In this sense, the realism of the drama articulates a knowing relationship between the viewer and the social world by activating a mental *mise-en-scène* of personal memory, recognition and perceptual familiarity. The stylised *neo-noir* sequences invoke a familiar generic landscape of theme and mood (corruption, misogyny, cynicism, alienation and violence), while the combination of atmospheric music and expressive camerawork creates a psychological landscape of personal desire and emotion, a critical characteristic of melodrama.

The playoff in the narrative structure of *Prime Suspect* is between the suspense generated by the game of detection (the story of the crime pieced together as the clues are revealed, the genre's oldest attribute) and the surprise of association created by female observation and deduction. Tennison not only solves crimes by making the links between the clues; her viewpoint reveals the personal and institutional misogyny that underpins both the committing of the crimes and the attempts to solve them. The series adopts a more psychological approach than previous action-based detective series such as *The Sweeney* and *The Professionals*; as well as humanising the detective by revealing her vulnerabilities, it shows her chief adversary and prime suspect George Marlow in a loving relationship with his common-law wife and caring for his elderly mother. This focus on psychologically plausible characters and their emotions shifts the generic realism of the British crime series away from the action-driven narratives of the 1970s and 1980s, creating a touchstone for subsequent series with a similar psychological focus such as *Between the Lines* (BBC 1 1992–4), *Cracker* (ITV 1993–6) and *Silent Witness* (BBC 1 1996–). Tennison's gender creates an added frisson in the battle of wits between the criminal investigator and her prime suspect as well as generating a mood of unease and resentment amongst the male detective team enhanced by *neo-noir* stylisation.

In contemporary Hollywood, *neo-noir* sexual themes are treated far more explicitly than in their 1940s and 1950s predecessors due to changing sexual mores and more relaxed attitudes to censorship.[9] In contrast, British television in the 1990s remained a highly regulated site with issues of taste and decency subject to codes of practice which, in the case of commercial television in the UK, were upheld by the Independent Television Commission (ITC).[10] The ITC banned the explicit depiction of sexual activity and personal violence, limiting what can be shown in the prime-time television crime series. In spite of the series' realist claims, explicit violence is shown in *Prime Suspect* only in one sequence, where a boxing match staged as part of a benefit night becomes an aggressive contest between two male policemen depicted in some detail – a way in which La Plante can demonstrate the testosterone-fuelled aggression of male police culture within the legitimate sphere of social rather than professional life. Sexual encounters are treated with similar discretion; although Tennison is shown in bed kissing and cuddling her lover, she is never depicted naked; in a similar manner, Marlow's sexual relations with his wife are hinted at rather than shown in graphic expositional detail. In line with this ethos of suggestion, there are no explicit depictions of the sexual violence inflicted on female victims, only the macabre photographic evidence of their mutilated dead bodies and the discovery of iron manacles bolted in the wall at the crime scene. The evidence is suggestive of sadistic tortures that the murder victims suffered, but there are no witnesses; viewers are left to imagine the graphic details for themselves.

In a discussion of the terms 'realism' and 'documentary' frequently used in press reviews of *Prime Suspect*, Jermyn (2003) points out that it was the graphic depiction of the dead victims' bodies and the recurrent use of their photographs that led many commentators to label the text as 'realist'. In spite of the series' restrained overall use of *vérité* style authenticity, the explicit depiction of dead bodies and the use of 'strong' language resulted in a number of complaints to the industry's watchdog the Broadcasting Standards Council. The complaints were not upheld because strong language was considered not inappropriate 'in the context of a play giving a realistic account of police investigations', and although the Council recognised 'the grimness of the spectacle of the bodies displayed' these images 'did not exceed limits reasonable in a drama of this sort' (Broadcasting Standards Council 1991 quoted by Jermyn 2003: 59). Jermyn points out how both the Broadcasting Standards Council and Granada, in their defence, draw upon comparisons between artistic production and 'real' life that situate this crime series in the tradition of the single play. It is unlikely however that La Plante would have been granted this 'licence to express an opinion' were not the graphic depictions of the dead bodies and the strong language in the text allied to the justified morality of Tennison's mission. Tennison's 'rightness', the 'truthfulness' of her position, depends not only upon the aesthetics of realism but on the use of narrative and the reconfiguration of the investigative structure of the television crime series.

Presented as a two-part four-hour mini-series broadcast over two consecutive nights, the form of the text allows a deeper examination of the psychological aspects of criminality than was common in crime series in the early 1990s. On one level the narrative is quite simple, replicating the pattern of criminal offence, investigation, pursuit and capture typical of the genre. A series of murders is committed and Tennison, pitting her mind against that of the killer, embarks on a mission to bring the perpetrator to justice. In crime thrillers there is a double plot often involving sexual desire and/or romance; in *film noir* variants this classically centres around an alienated male hero (often a private detective) and a woman who is an obstacle to his quest, her dangerous sexuality luring him into a web of corruption where solving the crime depends upon his ability to extricate himself from the spider-woman's clutches (Kaplan 1998: 2–3). In *Prime Suspect*, placing a woman in the central position as the investigator upsets the structural dynamics inherent in this form of the genre; instead of depicting the woman and her sexuality as a source of (male) intrigue and investiga-tion, male sexuality, masculinity and masculine structures of being and knowing become the focus of female interrogation. As Jane unfolds the story of the murders, she also discovers the corruption of her male superiors and colleagues; to solve the crime, she has to confront the problem of misogyny and corruption by overcoming the barriers erected to position her as an outsider and prevent her success. The terms on which she tackles these problems create the second plotline.

The second plotline of *Prime Suspect*, Tennison's desire for personal success and her exclusion from the all-male hierarchy of the police force, has evident parallels with the 'real' world and Alison Halford's case in particular. Tennison is the investigator of the murders but she herself is also the subject of investigation by the police force's male hierarchy, who keep her under strict surveillance and constantly threaten to remove her from the case unless she achieves a conviction. This is a very different depiction of the professional female police officer to the earlier 'humanist realism' of series such as *Cagney and Lacey*; as David Buxton points out, in *Cagney and Lacey* 'the effect of realism is obtained by foregrounding private life over police method'; this diminishes the drama's ability to comment on the social and economic crisis of the 1980s that was so relevant to the difficulties of policing (Buxton 1990: 139). Rather than focusing on Tennison's problems as 'women's problems' or displacing the social and economic problems of policing into the realm of personal crisis, La Plante draws on two traditionally 'masculine' forms of television drama to create an intervention not only in the generic dynamics of the crime series but in wider social, political and economic debates about sexual discrimina-tion in the workforce. One of these is rooted in a generic structure with which she is thoroughly familiar through her countless roles as prosti-tutes, dead and alive, in the crime series; the other is 'quality' drama, the legacy of the single play and the 'realism of record' with its authorial licence to 'voice an opinion' and its reputation for 'strategic penetra-tion'. The result is a star-led 'quality popular drama' that has strong resonances with the high production values of popular prime-time US crime series in the 1980s, such as *Hill Street Blues* (US MTM/C4 1981–9), combined with the contemporary address and depth of characterisation historically associated with the single play that in the 1980s became more prevalent in the mini-series and serial.

Glen Creeber argues that the drama serial became an ideal framework for integrating questions of social and political importance in the 1990s, using the example of *Prime Suspect* to point out how it investigates questions of power and politics on a number of different levels by integrating elements of the 'masculine' crime series and the 'feminine' soap opera within its narration. Tennison's working life is set firmly within the *mise-en-scène* of the crime series, while the problems she experiences with her partner and her personal life are framed within the domestic conventions of the soap opera. Both narratives take place 'in a wider *social* and *moral*' context that explores the institutional problems she encounters as one of the first female DCIs to run a murder investigation; the narratives come together in the mini-series' 'gradual exposition of the *domestic, institutional* and *generic* sexism it encounters and finally rejects'. For Creeber, the mini-series and the serial are able to explore the problems Tennison experiences on both 'a *micro-personal* level (the domestic sexism she faces at home) and a *macro-social* level (the institutional sexism she faces at work)' because the flexibility of serial form allows for greater complexity and flexibility of different layers of narrative within the episodic structure (italics in the original) (Creeber 2001c: 443).

In *Prime Suspect*, Tennison is initially marginalised by a male narrative of crime detection centred on DCI John Shefford (John Forgeham), a Jack Regan-like cop of the old school who relies on a mixture of intuition, bullying and luck to solve murders. The signifiers of *neo-noir* are clearly apparent in the opening sequence; a long shot of a dark urban street lit by pools of blue from the streetlights, the grainy image accompanied by an indistinct soundtrack of car radios, car doors slamming and men's voices. A handheld camera follows Shefford into the house and up the stairs, where he is taken on one side by Sergeant Bill Otley (Tom Bell), who covertly slips him a small black book. Close-ups of the murder victim's hands and feet are intercut with forensic activity as the pathologist recounts the physical condition of the body and possible cause of death; Shefford refuses to look at the dead woman's face, reinforcing the impression that something is amiss. The mutilated body is vividly displayed, the camera's lingering close-ups on the bruised and suppurating wrist wounds signalling a shift in the television crime series towards an increasingly graphic *mise-en-scène* that bears similarities to the use of observational realism in *Henry, Portrait of a Serial Killer* (McNaughton 1986). Based on the life of Henry Lee Lucas, who when he was only twenty-three years old confessed to killing three hundred and sixty people including his mother, the film provoked controversy when it was released in Britain in 1990, and was publicly defended by La Plante (Hallam with Marshment 2000: 229–40). If the style of *Prime Suspect* hints at its associations with horror films, it also makes strong claims to authenticity and verisimilitude in a similar manner to *Henry*; aspects of the narrative rapidly take on some of the characteristics and associations of a well-known dreadful reality, the serial murders committed by Peter Sutcliffe. the man dubbed by the tabloid press 'the Yorkshire Ripper'. Some but not all of the murdered women are prostitutes; they are murdered with a long thin instrument that the forensic pathologist suggests could be a sharpened Phillips screwdriver; there are multiple wounds on the women's breasts, abdomens and vaginas (Smith [1989] 1992 in Thornham 1994).

Shefford and his team begin the hunt for the killer; Tennison is metaphorically and literally marginalised, pushed to the back of the lift and ignored by the men shouting about beating Paxman's record as they attempt to convict the killer in under thirty-six hours. As time begins to run out on Shefford's self-appointed deadline, he has a cardiac arrest and subsequently dies. Risking alienation from all around her, Tennison seizes the opportunity to take over the murder enquiry, insisting that the case is rightfully hers, that she was on duty on the night of the murder and has been by-passed once too often; begrudgingly she is permitted by her superiors to step into the dead man's shoes. The tension in the incident room is palpable as Tennison confronts the team for the first time with the information that the victim has been misidentified. Shefford's former associate and close friend Sergeant Bill Otley is hostile and unhelpful, undermining Tennison's authority with insults and barbed comments designed to publicly humiliate her. In a concerted effort to break her confidence, undermine her leadership and have her removed from the case he addresses the team with an stream of vitriolic abuse about Tennison's working methods that includes terms such as 'tart', 'skinny arsed bitch' and 'dyke'. Tennison is only able to quell the venomous insults and end Otley's campaign of non-cooperation by resorting to underhand bargaining tactics. When she discovers he has hidden vital evidence in order to conceal Shefford's sexual relationships with two of the murdered women, she uses it to blackmail the support of senior officers and silence Otley. She quickly learns that she cannot play by the rules and hope to win; the odds are stacked too heavily against her.

Tennison's efforts to solve the murder unveil a network of corrupt practices and blatant misogyny within the police force itself; the dead Shefford's diary reveals that he knows the murdered prostitutes and seems to be implicated in the crimes, becoming in Tennison's eyes a potential prime suspect, suspicions that she can only share with her male colleagues if she is prepared to sacrifice her own career ambitions. Tennison's personal investigation of the corruption within the force parallels the official surveillance under which she is kept; because she is regarded as a potential threat to masculine autonomy and police authority she has to be contained. Tennison is the first character in a police series to investigate the masculine ethos of police subculture and its consequences for those 'outside' the accepted image of the male police officer, the first to question an internal value system that contravenes the formal rule of law by ignoring equal opportunities legislation and looking after its own. *Prime Suspect* shows that women can be good police officers, overcoming the obstacles created by a masculine subculture that defines its masculinity in terms of the dominant (hegemonic) values associated with conflict, daring and white male supremacy (Eaton 1995: 166). Those who do not conform in their appearance or behaviour to these masculinist, patriarchal ideals, be they women, homosexual or racially different, are perceived as outsiders, 'others'. Tennison's segregation and exclusion from the male 'club' is presented throughout in these terms – through sexist comments, non-cooperation from the team and her lack of socialising in the pub after work.

Visually there is a clear demarcation between images that depict Tennison in combat with her male colleagues in a '*noiresque*' landscape devoid, of colour and detail and sequences where she is more at home in her domestic space, in her personal relations and in the everyday work of police enquiry, of questioning witnesses and demanding answers. As well as the bleak images drained of colour in the grey rooms and corridors of the police station, allusions to the *noir* tradition are scattered throughout the text. The prime suspect's name is George Marlow (John Bowe), linking him to the character of the private investigator Philip Marlowe memorably played by 1940s star Humphrey Bogart in one of the most popular adaptations of the hard-boiled detective novels by Raymond Chandler, *The Big Sleep* (1946). Philip Marlow (Michael Gambon) is also the name given to Dennis Potter's disfigured and ailing writer in *The Singing Detective*, a character who is unable to separate his misogynistic fantasies of women as sexual sirens, seductresses and prostitutes from their everyday social reality as nurses and from his girlfriend (Creeber 2001a). In contrast to the unattractive figure of the writer in Potter's fictional world, George Marlow's matinee-idol looks are a magnet for women; his former boss comments on how women love him and it seems that Marlow shares a similar love of women. Marlow makes no secret of his sexual predilection for prostitutes (his common-law wife Moyra (Zoe Wanamaker) is a former prostitute), but denies this interest is anything other than healthy sexual pleasure. The image constructed of George, unlike the cold-blooded emotionless character of Henry Lee Lucas in *Henry, Portrait of a Serial Killer*, is of a man wrongly accused and hounded by police who are determined to make a quick arrest regardless of the lack of evidence.

It is Marlow's partner Moyra who makes the first direct reference to the drama's *film noir* roots. In recounting a story of early embarrassment and shame, Marlow describes how his mother's wig blew off when she visited him at school: 'underneath all that glamour, she was ugly, like she was someone I never knew'. Moyra retorts, 'The Rita Hayworth of Warrington was really Yul Brynner in disguise', evoking the name of a 1940s star who played classic *femmes fatales*. If Marlow's mother is not what she appears to be, the use of the mirror shot, a classic *noir* signifier of female duplicity (Place 1978: 35–40), throws doubt upon Moyra; after she is interrogated by the police, the camera captures her reflection as she cleanses her face in the mirror. The self-absorbed narcissism with which Moyra removes her makeup implies that from now on she will be looking after herself; the split frame suggests that neither Moyra nor Marlow can be trusted. In spite of growing suspicions about Marlow's guilt, he is afforded a depth of character usually denied the villains of crime series, enhancing his credibility as a flawed but not abnormal man. It is only in the final session in the interview room with Tennison that his boyish demeanour cracks, his rage revealing an oedipal obsession with his mother that has become a common theme in crime thrillers since Hitchcock's *Psycho* (1960).

In the 'feminine' space of her kitchen, with its golden pine cupboards and soft yellow light, Tennison is revealed as a more domesticated, softer person than is usual in crime series. This depiction of the gentler side of her character is tinged with the warm glow of nostalgia for a haven of domestic bliss that only exists in fantasies; the kitchen rapidly becomes the setting for disaster as she distractedly tries to please her live-in lover Tom. The first indication that work and domestic life are doomed not to mix occurs when she endearingly covers her stark white work blouse in chocolate sauce while preparing to entertain Tom's young son. Tom, although initially appearing as a new man who shares childcare with his ex-wife, has little sympathy with Tennison's career ambitions; his principal concern is his own ailing business. Tennison's absorption in her first murder case leads to conflict; Tom leaves when she fails to arrive home in time to cook a meal and entertain his business associates. These domestic images of interpersonal struggle are in stark contrast to the formal confrontations in the incident room;

addressing the dark-suited men wearing black ties as a mark of respect to their dead colleague, Tennison stands against a background of photographs of the mutilated bodies of the dead women. With her short blonde hair, white blouse and dark skirt, she appears cold, clinical and businesslike, devoid of emotion, but the stark visual contrasts are a reminder of the different narratives at stake. Have the murdered women scattered across the *noir* landscape found their Nemesis? Or will ambition seduce Tennison and compromise her professionalism, luring her into the network of corruption and amorality typical of the classic *noir* thriller?

In *Prime Suspect 2 noir* stylisation gives way to generic realism, perhaps because the underlying premise of *noir*, that 'blackness' is a fall from the purity of 'whiteness', was deemed stylistically inappropriate for a subject as sensitive as racism in the police force (see, for example, Diawara 1993). The drama pre-dates the McPherson enquiry into police practices and procedures which concluded that racism was endemic in police culture, but not the growing swell of disquiet in the media concerning the numbers of young black men dying in police custody.[11] Much to Tennison's embarrassment as she has recently had a one-night stand with him at a conference, DS Oswalde (Colin Salmon) is drafted onto Tennison's team to assist with a racially sensitive murder enquiry. The subplot hinges upon Oswalde's desire as a young black British policeman for acceptance in the force and Tennison's desire as a white middle-class woman for promotion while at the same time indulging her desire to know the 'other' for reasons that have little to do with love. Oswalde's presence reveals racial prejudice and racialised attitudes in Tennison as well as her team, attitudes which are questioned but resolved at a personal rather than an institutional level, leaving the hegemonic culture of white masculinity in the police force largely absolved of criticism and blame.

There is the same attention to narrative detail in Tennison's determined quest not only to uncover the murderer but to probe her own and her colleagues' prejudices in *Prime Suspect 2*, but the camerawork remains at a safe mid- to long-shot distance from its subjects and is noticeably less engaged with characters' faces, an approach that creates a loss of emotional intensity and focus. Although the camera creates an initial alignment with Oswalde's point of view as he enters the incident room and meets a sea of white faces, much in the way that we are initially positioned with Tennison's viewpoint in the first series, this drama is for the most part un-involving – perhaps because there are no generic short-hands to exemplify racial alienation and exclusion in the way that *noir* stylisation conventionally (and conveniently) references the existential angst and corruption of its white male heroes. The atten-tion given to intricate plotting and the detailed minutiae of police work shifts the stylistic register away from the implication that racism is a form of endemic institutional corruption towards a more sociological 'procedural' focus on police methods and practices. Tennison fails to get her promotion but Oswalde does eventually get his man after he has undertaken a ritualistic journey of transformation and initiation into white institutional culture that effectively kills his 'black self' in much the same way that Tennison becomes progressively 'masculinised' as she becomes accustomed to being in charge. Before hanging himself in a police cell, while under interrogation Oswalde's prime suspect Tony Allen reminds Oswalde that assimilation has its price; Oswalde survives the ordeal of the ensuing inquest and is free to pursue the prime suspect, but denies his own complicity in the innocent man's death. As is so frequently the case in television drama, the problems of institu-tional racism are represented by the attitudes and prejudices of a few unreformed individuals rather than, as in the first *Prime Suspect*, through a depiction of systemic corruption created by the damaging and destructive force of white male police culture.

Transmitted in 1993, *Prime Suspect 3* (directed by David Drury) has a similar structure to the first *Prime Suspect* and a similar visual style, evoking a male world of unlawful desire through its focus on the death of a rent boy in a suspected case of arson. Investigation of the death reveals the existence of a male prostitute and paedophile ring protected from investigation by the membership of high-ranking police officers and other figures in authority. The contemporary dimensions of this story are drawn from accounts of male rape in local authority children's homes that led to the eventual closure of numerous institutions in England and Wales and the prosecution of some of the perpetrators. Over a number of years it became clear that there was widespread, systematic abuse of boys and young men in local authority institutions whose ostensible purpose was to protect them from harm and care for them; the abusers were members of paedophile networks protected by people in authority.[12] Tennison's mission in this series is to clean up Soho; her personal quest is to get a result and achieve promotion but she is also depicted as a woman at a personal crossroads in her life when she discovers that she is pregnant. Her personal desire for children in a stable relationship of trust and mutual respect – a desire she feels is totally unrealistic – is cross-cut with the fate of the boys on the streets, unwanted children left to fend for themselves in a twilight zone of male violence, sexually transmitted disease and gross exploitation.

The opening sequence again sets a *neo-noir* tone, cutting between a cabaret act in a sleazy nightclub where a drag queen disguised as Marlene Dietrich (Peter Capaldi) performs a camp rendition of 'Falling in Love Again' while a young thug (David Thewlis) chases a terrified pre-pubescent boy through dimly lit back streets. The stylised framing depicts a Dickensian London, an underworld of street urchins and rent boys terrorised by pimps living amidst poverty and AIDS and, as the narrative slowly reveals, betrayed by the social workers who are paid to help them. Sergeant Otley, Tennison's misogynistic adversary from the first *Prime Suspect*, works with her rather than against her this time after she clearly states at the beginning of the investigation, 'I'm not taking any more crap from you Sergeant'. By now Tennison is more confident and self-assertive; she is not just 'one of the lads' but in control of her team, able to negotiate the misogynistic and homophobic attitudes of those under her command. In this atmosphere of greater tolerance created by her leadership, DI Ray Hebdon (Mark Drewry) 'comes out', announcing his homosexuality to the rest of team and at the same time supplying them with vital information. He also confronts the irrational homophobia of a former friend and colleague, DI Brian Dalton (Andrew Doodall). Dalton is seconded from head office to keep an eye on Tennison, who is once again under surveillance to prevent her from uncovering internal corruption. Out on a police raid, Dalton is bitten by a young witness with AIDS; Tennison takes time to offer him guidance and support, knowing he is a 'plant', there to prevent her revealing links between the young male prostitutes and high-ranking officers. Her care and respect for others – the abused children, a transsexual witness, members of the team – is cross-cut with the discovery that she is pregnant and her decision to have an abortion. The pleasures and difficulties of personal mothering are rejected in favour of social mothering; nurturing her 'boys' to become better policemen and citizens and, by definition, more compassionate men. In this sense, Tennison is an agent of reform, challenging outmoded notions of Masonic fidelity through a slow process of incorporation and change. Such processes always risk contamination and corruption – in this case that the 'feminine' values of care and concern will be absorbed into 'masculine' discourses of professionalism that ultimately serve to protect the privilege of white male middle-class agency.[13]

La Plante's reconfiguration of the crime series is beyond doubt; whether her intervention is a feminist one remains open to debate. Tennison is an unusual female character because her personal desires for fulfilment are focused on her public role and status rather than her private life, on satisfying her mind rather than being ruled by her body. She is not driven by traditionally ascribed 'feminine' desires that situate a personal life of mothering and family duty as her most important responsibilities but by a fierce determination to achieve recognition in the public sphere in her chosen career. As an enforcer of the dominant status quo in a conventional law and order narrative, her desire for individual success marks her as a liberal feminist, someone who is determined to succeed on her own account, who makes no change to the structure or the ethos of the institutions with which she engages. Other interpretations of her character might emphasise how, if she is to be plausibly successful in her ambitions, she has to be shown to take on and engage with male-dominated working practices on her own terms; as one of very few women in a masculine environment, she has to persuade her male colleagues to have confidence in her if she wants to survive.

Similarly to her character, before La Plante can change the crime genre she has to infiltrate its working practices, which in this case entails shifting the androcentric discourse of the law and order narrative, with its personal ethos of bullying and intuitive individualism, towards a more professional form of practice in which attention to detail is of prime importance. Detail is often associated with femininity, particularly in discourses about the difference between 'fine' arts like painting and the 'decorative' arts such as embroidery. Naomi Schor, for example, argues that certain Dutch painters were excluded from the Great Tradition because their work was based on the detailed observation of particularities (a form of naturalism), whereas in traditional evaluations of aesthetics, 'Genius consists principally in the comprehension of a whole' (Schor in Caughie 2000a: 167). Caughie draws on Schor's analysis of the distinctions between these two creative modes to discuss the relationship between detail and femininity as it is manifest in acting (Schor in Caughie 2000a). Detail is associated with the domestic, the everyday and the ornamental, all characteristics traditionally associated with the feminine. La Plante's attention to the minutiae of detail in her research, her incorporation of the detail of police procedure in her writing and Mirren's interpretation of the emotional detail of Tennison's character in her acting 'feminise' a form previously preoccupied with the machismo of gun-toting detectives and car chases. This attention to detail is evident in Mirren's performance and Tennison's actions; her thorough combing of the files, her scrupulous examination of the victims' clothing, her attention to photographic detail, her skill of listening to the less confident members of her team. In *Prime Suspect 2*, the unidentified dead body is thought initially to be that of a missing local girl; Tennison assembles a series of personal items and clothing found with the body, including among them her own watch, and asks the mother if she can identify them. The distraught woman claims that all the items belonged to her missing daughter including the watch, a misidentification that enables Tennison to discount the body as that of the missing girl. It is this kind of attention to detail that shifts the generic register of *Prime Suspect* away from associations with the masculine ethos of 'intuitive' crime detection embodied in Shefford and Otley towards an intellectual, rational depiction of 'the feminine'.

A further shift is embodied in the character of Tennison and the role as played by Helen Mirren. The atmosphere of menace, of a hidden underworld of corruption, is used to situate Jane as a moral agent, a reforming woman, her prim sensibilities reflected in the clothes she wears, her dark suits, high-necked white blouses and low-heeled shoes bearing, as Sue Thornham (1994) has pointed out, a marked similarity to the dress of Margaret Thatcher. But Tennison is not like Margaret Thatcher, even though she has to work in an environment where the males often behave like truculent schoolboys while policewomen end-lessly shift the paperwork (represented literally as they carry armfulls of files around in the background); nor is she, as she remarks in frustra-tion to one of the lads who insists on calling her Ma'am, 'the bloody queen'. Her clothing marks out her difference, her femininity (she never wears trousers), but it also functions in a similar way to a uni-form, a form of protective clothing that signifies her respectability and moral agency in the way that nurses' uniforms serve the double function of distinguishing them from other women and acting as literal and metaphorical barriers to physical and psychic contamination (Hallam 2000a: 133–42). Tennison's clothes help her to project an attitude of professional disinterest and detachment in situations where she has to cope with rotting corpses, putrefying flesh, potentially sadistic murderers and distraught relatives. Her subdued designer clothes are also a mark of her class and status in confrontations where women do not com-mand public confidence, as her boss Detective Superintendent Kernan (John Benfield) constantly reminds her. Clothes are the mark of differ-ence used by Hannibal Lecter (Antony Hopkins) in *Silence of the Lambs* to remind Clarice Starling that she is trailer trash, her cheap bag and makeup marking her out as a woman from the wrong side of the tracks; Tennison's designer clothes are worn as a protective barrier to signify class difference and middle-class respectability. Here, as in other aspects of Mirren's performance, attention to detail of makeup and accessories is of prime importance. Tennison's constant awareness of herself as an image is foregrounded in the sequence where she appears on *Crime Night*, a sequence intercut with scenes of other people watch-ing her – her family, her lover, Otley amidst the male camaraderie of the boxing night benefit match for Shefford, the dead girl's parents, and Marlow and his common-law wife Moyra. La Plante claims that it was the BBC's *Crime Watch* programme that made her aware of the lack of female detectives; all the police representatives that appeared on the programmes were male (Purser 1991). Mirren makes Tennison's consciousness of the importance of her appearance a central concern; she is the first female detective to appear in public in this way and the response to her request for witnesses will depend on how seriously people take her, which depends in part on her ability to look professional but not intimidating. She abandons her usual dark suit for a lighter one, is careful to apply just the right amount of makeup to her define her as 'feminine' but not too much makeup or she will be defined, in Otley's words, as a tart; if she wears no makeup at all, she risks being labelled a 'dyke' and a man hater.

In this sense, her appearance is less a disguise or a 'mask of femininity' than a strategic tool that she uses to exemplify her respectability and her class status, underlining the argument made by feminist sociologists such as Beverly Skeggs (1997) that femininity functions similarly to class as a social discourse that constructs and defines female identity. In the crime series this definition traditionally turned on the relationship between 'respectable' women such as wives and girlfriends who rely on their male partners' status for economic and social security, and prostitutes, who rely on their bodies as the economic capital that enables them to earn a living. 'Working girls' such as policewomen often tread a thin line between the two, a relationship that is often made apparent in crime series through policewomen masquerading as prostitutes as part of vice squad clean-up operations (Tasker 1998: 89–115). Tennison avoids this particular charade, although she is misrecognised as a prostitute when she interviews two associates of one of the murdered prostitutes in the first *Prime Suspect*, a misunderstanding that causes amusement and sisterly comradeship until Tennison announces she will be late for the dinner party she is organising for her live-in lover, re-establishing the class and status boundaries between them.

It is not Tennison's appearance, however, that gives her 'balls', as her commander puts it. She is not a man in drag, in spite of her plain suits, low-key makeup and adopting certain behaviours often coded as 'masculine' such as smoking, drinking and swearing. It is her capacity to stand up for herself, to not 'whinge and whine' about her women's rights, to demand the attention of those she works with and to achieve her aims on her own terms that commands male respect. She sees things from a different perspective and it is this perspective, her female gaze, that enables her to correctly identify the body at the beginning of the first *Prime Suspect*; examining the victim's clothes, she notes that they are expensive, designer clothes, not the kind of clothes a 'working girl' like Della Mornay would normally afford. She listens to people, in particular her female police constable assistant WPC Maureen Havers (Mossie Smith) and her tentative suggestions concerning a possible connection between Moyra's trade in 'nu-nails' and the false nails worn by several of the victims. There is even a sense of Tennison's 'sister-hood' with other women in the glances that cut across barriers of rank and class, such as those between Tennison and WPC Havers and between Tennison and the prostitutes in the final courtroom scene.

A similar relay of looks occurs in *Prime Suspect 2* between Tennison and Sarah Allen (Jenny Jules), the sister of a man who has died in police custody. Both women have become the object of the murdering porno-grapher's gaze: Jane is photographed on her doorstep giving Oswalde a goodnight kiss, an indiscretion that will cost her the promotion she is so keen to achieve when the photographs appear in the tabloid newspapers the following day. Sarah is photographed undressing in her room and receives the prints with a letter that threatens to harm her if she implicates the pornographer in her account of the events leading to the murder that she witnessed. A trainee lawyer, Sarah realises she can no longer live in fear and takes the photographs to Tennison, who persuades her to reveal the information that will convict her prime suspect. As in the first series the conviction depends on women overcoming their differences to find and punish those who commit crimes against women; Moyra Henson will only reveal her evidence in the presence of Tennison and WPC Havers, insisting that all the men, including her lawyer, leave the room. The relay of looks between the women cements their solidarity, marking this out as 'women's business'. Sue Thornham argues that these looks are in marked contrast to institutional forms of looking such as surveillance (including that of Tennison herself by her superiors), autopsy, photographic evidence and the unlawful looks of the pornographer that characterise the masculine world. They provide Tennison with support and relay the look of the viewer through feminine (and potentially feminist) forms of viewing pleasure (Thornham 1994: 231).

The allegiances between women in the *Prime Suspect* series are not simple stories of female solidarity, however; although they sometimes transcend barriers of racial, class and sexual difference, primarily they create an ambivalence about the relations between women and the institutions of law and order. In *Prime Suspect 3*, Tennison forms a gendered alliance with the transsexual Vera although by this time she is expressing less solidarity with her female colleagues, a theme continued in *Prime Suspect 4: Inner Circles* (written by Eric Deacon), in which she testily warns the young female Detective Sergeant Chris Cromwell (Sophie Stanton) not to expect any favours from her because of her gender. Nonetheless, an uneasy allegiance is forged; DS Cromwell is a working-class girl with aspirations to do well in her profession: she helps Tennison root out the prime suspect, this time a female solicitor. As the series progresses, Tennison's determination to deal with the politics of both the old boys' network and the lads in her team results in an increasing obsession with promotion that implies, as Thornham suggests, that she is no longer 'sleeping with the enemy but married to the job' (Thornham 1994). Tennison's gender becomes less of an issue as she is incorporated slowly into the systems, both generic and institutional, that Lynda La Plante, in the first three series, so effectively challenged.

Acting, Authorship and Stardom

> There is no question that Jane is the most successful character I've created. I get very emotional about anything of mine, every character I create but Jane is the one who opened doors for me. (La Plante in Day-Lewis 1998: 85)

At the time *Prime Suspect* was made Lynda La Plante was insufficiently famous or critically acclaimed to be publicised as the author of the series by placing her name in a prominent position 'above the line'. The name singled out is that of Helen Mirren, an established British actress known in theatrical circles for her work on the stage and in British feature films, among which her performances in *The Long Good Friday* (Mackenzie 1980) and the controversially acclaimed *The Cook, The Thief, His Wife and Her Lover* (Greenaway 1989) earned her an international reputation and a Cannes critics award. Situated towards the 'high' end of the popular culture/high culture continuum, Mirren's status as a performer embraces both the serious and the sexy. An RSC actress, she is also known for taking off her clothes and could be termed 'the thinking man's pin-up' or as she has commented herself, the 'RSC's sex queen' or 'the thinking thespian's tea-cake', implying the possibility of more fluid identifications across gender boundaries (Garfield 1990). The success of *Prime Suspect* shifted Mirren's 'star' appeal from the thespian margins to centre stage; DCI Jane Tennison stands as an icon of change in female characterisation in popular television drama, registering the shift in the representation of women from secondary characters to the central roles they now commonly occupy in many prime-time series and serials.

A closer analysis of the ways in which Mirren's success is evaluated reveals that in addition to her sex appeal she is respected for her acting ability, which is invariably assessed according to humanistic critical concerns such as realism, authenticity and truth, evaluations which rest on judgements of how well the actor in John Caughie's words 'en-acts and em-bodies feelings *as if* they were real in a way which makes them real for them and for us' (Caughie 2000b: 164). Here I want to explore the tension between Mirren's public image, her star persona and her acting, and the relationship of these aspects of her career to the character who has become an iconic representation of the professional woman in the workplace in the early 1990s. The account is informed by the concept of television authorship as a collective enterprise, one in which the actor, as the creator of the performance that we see on the screen, is often better known than the writer who created the role or the director who films the work, particularly in multi-authored series and serials where the technical crew and the actors often provide the continuity that enables character development within the generic constraints of recognisable story structures and themes.

Created a dame in 2003, Helen Mirren is recognised as an actor at the top of her profession in the UK, amidst others renowned for their acting skills such as Judi Dench, Diana Rigg and Joan Plowright. Unlike many notable British actors who have found fame and stardom in Hollywood, Mirren has spent the majority of her working life in the UK, appearing in films and stage productions as well as television drama. Since the demise of the British film industry's contract system in the early 1960s, the notion of a British star tends to be reserved for actors who 'cross the pond' to work in Hollywood, such as Ewan McGreggor and Catherine Zeta Jones, and, by virtue of the success of the films they appear in, become known internationally. Hollywood stardom has eluded Mirren, although she spends much of her time in Los Angeles with her partner, film director Taylor Hackford. Reportedly she has some regrets about this; when in 1994 it was proposed to make *Prime Suspect* into a film the press commented on Mirren's 'fury' that Hollywood stars with guaranteed box-office appeal such as Jane Fonda and Meryl Streep were being considered for role she had created (Mirren 1994).

Nonetheless, the distinction between a celebrity actor such as Mirren and a star is not always a clear one. Barry King suggests that the ability to 'impersonate' a character rather than 'personify' a character foregrounds dramatic acting ability as the basis of character differentiation, while a star's public image may override differences between the characters that they play (King 1991: 168). Many contemporary film stars blur this distinction, however, by acting in off-Broadway and West End stage theatre productions and are keen to be recognised for their talent as actors, not only as stars. Most academic writing on acting and stardom focuses on the film industry; acting in television drama has received very little critical attention, perhaps because, as Caughie suggests, 'the actor acting is a messily humanist component of the specific signifying practices of film and television, a kind of impressionistic marshland' (Caughie 2000b: 163). At the risk of getting caught up in this mess, I want to suggest that it is Mirren's performance, her ability to convince us that the character she portrays could be 'real', that makes Jane Tennison and the *Prime Suspect* series so memorable.

Following her success in *Prime Suspect*, in 1994 Mirren returned to the stage to play Natalya Petrovna in a West End production of Turgenev's *A Month in the Country*, a play that formed part of the repertoire of the Moscow Arts Theatre. Formed in 1897 under the directorship of Constantin Stanislavski, the Moscow Arts Theatre is credited with the development of nineteenth-century stage realism and what was at the time a new style of acting centred on the detailed depiction of character psychology and emotion. This style contrasted with popular stage melodrama, which with its stock characters and gestures that relied on a formulaic catalogue of movements and expressions to illustrate emotional states became a low-brow form of entertainment. Realism, meanwhile, was a barometer of middle-class distinction and taste. The notion of constructing a character that is psychologically plausible is central to the realist project and one of its principal sources of pleasure. Criticised by twentieth-century modernists and constructivists such as Eisenstein and Brecht for its bourgeois sensibilities and its inability to reveal the artifice of its representational strategies, realism continues to be the dominant mode of expression in western cultures in film and television drama as well as on the stage. Within this context, Stanislavski's Method, a system for training actors that teaches them to draw on their personal experiences as the basis of the character they are expressing, continues to inform contemporary ideas about authenticity of performance and characterisation.[14]

It is unsurprising to find that critical assessments of Mirren's stage performance judge it in these 'messily humanist' terms: Benedict Nightingale in *The Times*, for example, comments:

> Turgenev's wordy but acute play requires his Natalya ... to shift from emotion to emotion more rapidly than any character in drama. Helen Mirren rises to the challenge brilliantly, constructing a seamless psychological garment from what might have been patches only. (Nightingale 1994)

Casting Mirren, an actor with expertise in the detailed depiction of psychologically realised characters, in a role traditionally associated with the goal-driven machismo of the detective hero epitomised by John Shefford in *Prime Suspect* brings what John Caughie (2000b) argues is a 'feminine' tradition of acting associated with 'quality' literary adaptations into the 'masculine' terrain of the crime series. Traditionally, the intimate and domestic nature of television has encouraged a propensity to create 'personalities' rather than stars; it therefore follows that television acting seems to favour impersonation rather than personification. Impersonation implies a game of pretence, of playing the part as if the person is real; in mini-series and serials the extended format can offer an actor more scope to develop their character in this way than in the two-hour format of a feature film or a stage production. Mirren's portrayal of Tennison in the initial series of *Prime Suspect* arguably falls into the category of impersonation; in the early days of playing the character, she often made comments that disassociated herself from the role, claiming that although she admired Tennison she didn't like her.

If television acting favours impersonation rather than personification, the extended narrative formats of mini-series and serials allow a more in-depth focus on the psychological detail of performance rather than the narrative function of the role. The decision to structure the early series of *Prime Suspect* as a four-hour mini-series broadcast in two-hour slots on consecutive nights had implications for Mirren's performance. She was able to develop depth and detail of characterisation that arguably counteracts the segmented flow of the drama created by advertising breaks. John Caughie argues that British television drama has evolved 'as a drama of incident and character rather than as a kind of ruthlessly driven goal-orientated narrative which is associated with classic Hollywood cinema' (2000b: 166). It is possible to distinguish between acting that 'is cut to the measure of narrative and acting which goes beyond, offering an excess of detail at the service of the intricacy and complexity of character' (2000b: 169). This suggests a useful way of analysing Mirren's performance and the ways in which it 'real-ises' and materialises the practice of misogyny. Such a critique must be grounded in affect, in the ways in which Mirren *as if* she is Tennison has to cope with and emotionally respond to the day-to-day sexism she experiences in the workplace.

The first time Tennison decides to assertively challenge her marginalised status is in a meeting with her boss DCS Kernan (John Benfield) following the death of John Shefford; the sequence depicts Tennison's nervousness as approaches his office door, a feeling conveyed in the way she holds her mouth and raises her chin as she approaches the door

(Figure 1), running her hands through her hair and adjusting her blouse as she collects and contains herself before knocking and entering (Figure 2). The encounter begins in a friendly fashion but rapidly becomes combative as she demands, as Kernan puts it, her 'women's rights'. Mirren/Tennison sits facing Kernan across his desk perched on the edge of her upright chair; he leans back in a relaxed fashion in his office recliner (Figure 3); after an initial classic two shot with both characters in profile divided by the desk, the camera switches to a mid shot–reverse shot sequence moving into close-up as the tension mounts between them (Figure 4). Having accepted a cigarette from Kernan, Mirren uses it to punctuate her verbal points, accentuating Tennison's growing agitation; she looks Kernan in the eye throughout (Figure 5). Refusing to accept his decision to bring in an outsider to lead the case, she stands her ground and presses her argument, leaning forward in the chair, her jaw set more forward, teeth closer together; the impression she creates is one of tightly controlled anger. She drops her gaze as Kernan refuses her request, then, contravening conventional politeness and expected feminine behaviour, looks him straight in the eye again as the meeting ends before she turns her back on him and leaves the room (Figure 6).

A similarly intense impression of constrained nervous tension is conveyed through Mirren's tightly controlled performance of Tennison's first encounter with her team as head of the murder squad. Delivering her introduction in a calm and professional manner, she is interrupted by Shefford's former associate Otley. Responding to this first attempt to undermine her authority, the tip of Mirren's tongue hovers between her lips as if she is biting her tongue (Figure 7) to avoid saying something she knows she will regret; she then proceeds to present a summary of the evidence gathered so far and to announce the misidentification of the victim, aware of the steely reception from the team. At the end of the briefing the camera tracks backwards, recording Mirren's exit from the incident room, cutting to a medium close-up as she leaves and closes the door (Figure 8); she leans against it, shutting her eyes and opening her mouth to draw a deep breath of relief (Figure 9), then lights a cigarette and draws a draught of stress-relieving smoke into her lungs (Figure 10). She may be brave and assertive but Mirren depicts Tennison as someone who is also quite vulnerable and very much alone. Mirren's performance is embellished throughout with these small details, furnishing Tennison's character with emotional responses, depicting the effort she has to make to act as a cool-headed professional in situations where she is consistently undermined by the men she has to work with. She cannot just get on with her job and,

Prime Suspect, ITV (Granada) 1991
DCI Tennison – Helen Mirren, DCS Michael Kiernon – John Benfield. Directed by
Christopher Menaul.

7

8

9

10

unlike the men, has little support from her female colleagues even though they are all subordinate to her.

Mirren's performance, in tandem with the camerawork, supports and extends La Plante's script by providing an in-depth and sustained critique of the material and psychological effects of sexual discrimination in the workplace. Like La Plante, Mirren researched the role by talking to and studying female police officers and their body language; she was told never to fold her arms because it is a defensive action. Such attention to small gestures and facial expressions builds a complex impression of Tennison as a character that offers viewers a range of interpretative possibilities from awareness of Mirren's acting skills and pleasure in watching her performance to an enjoyment of her representation of the 'new woman' detective of the 1990s who, like her female antecedents in the crime novel, demands to be recognised for her intellectual abilities, her attention to detail and her capacity for decisive action.

Mirren's performance in *Prime Suspect* changed her public image from accomplished actress and erotic object of middle-class desire to that of popular television personality and 'star'. In the press she was critically lauded for her ability to project a significant image of contemporary female identity in emotive rather than propagandistic terms, although feminist responses were rather more guarded. Sue Thornham (1994), for example, argues that Mirren's popular image constrains the potentially subversive meanings of *Prime Suspect* and its critique of patriarchal culture within a safe discourse of liberal feminism; agency is granted to the individual but the deeper structures of the genre and the institutions it represents are left untouched. Drawing on the publicity coverage for the first *Prime Suspect*, Thornham suggests that most of the press and magazine commentary works actively to redefine both the character and the meaning of the text by emphasising Mirren's (hetero) sexuality and femininity. In the *Radio Times* she was promoted as 'an actress more readily associated with sex than Shakespeare'. The *TV Times* quotes Mirren as saying, 'I tried to get a little sexuality into the part of Jane ... after all, she's a woman'; to Mirren's observation, 'After all ... you can't keep playing girls or women of a certain type', it adds the comment, 'The most familiar type being the clothes-tearing-off, anytime-anyplace-anywhere mistress she played in *The Cook, The Thief, His Wife and Her Lover*'. *What's On* quotes the actor who played serial killer George Marlow: 'Helen's a total sex bomb off-screen and on', while publicity photos show Mirren sexually posed with film director Taylor Hackford, a reminder that in spite of her independent status, she has now found fulfilment 'in the longest relationship of her life' (*TV Times*).¹⁵ Thornham argues that if 'such "inter-textual" redefinitions act as "supervisory discourses" seeking to contain potential subversive readings of the text, the attempt here is clearly to reaffirm conventional notions of femininity' (Thornham 1994: 228–9).

The struggle to contain the character within this discourse hinges on the relationship between Mirren's star persona, her performance and the interpretation of her character. 'What kind of woman are you'? asks the boyfriend of one of the murdered women as he bears the brunt of Tennison's assertive and probing questions in the interview room. As well as being bluntly businesslike in emotionally sensitive situations, Tennison smokes and drinks whisky, swears on occasion and deems her own ambitions more important than supporting her partner's business life or attending her father's birthday party, egotistical and selfish characteristics which confound expectations governing 'feminine' behaviour. She is considered by her colleagues unnecessarily aggressive, pursuing lines of questioning that upset the acquaintances of the victims, and insensitive, insisting on her authority to lead a murder enquiry to the victim's father who is suffering from severe shock. Examining mutilated and sometimes putrefying bodies at crime scenes, in the mortuary and at autopsies, her ability to look at the faces of the dead women is unflinchingly dispassionate, a trait which is normally socially gendered as 'masculine'. In contrast to these 'masculine' attitudes and behaviours, her performance is manifestly 'feminine' in its gestural and signifying codes; although her questioning is direct and to the point, her manner is that of a calm, reserved and self-possessed woman, not a bullying, aggressive and physically threatening one. The two aspects of her physical self through which she sometimes reveals her vulnerability are distinctly feminine: her gaze is frequently unwavering and direct and her body language – particularly the ways in which she uses her hands and face, moves and occupies space within the frame – demonstrates a quiet confidence and self-contained assertiveness. In spite of her inner tension, she rarely raises her voice or displays fits of aggressive temper or excessive emotion; as Brunsdon (1998) notes, the only time she is noticeably moved to tears is when she is accepted by the squad as 'one of the boys'. Her personal life is similarly marked by a lack of emotional displays with her male partners, yet she is affectionate and responds sexually to men; she is not a cold or frigid woman. She appears genuinely to want to support her live-in lover in spite of what he defines as her 'excessive' involvement in her work, an involvement also judged by some feminists as a 'masculine' trait.

Mirren herself has often voiced reservations about the character: 'Tennison is a driven, obsessive, vulnerable, unpleasantly egotistical and confused woman. But she is damn good at what she does and totally dedicated' (Hayward and Rennert 1996: 14). At the same time, she thinks of her as a good friend:

> When I start to play her again after a period away, it's as if I'm coming back to someone I know quite well ... I would never have said it's a part that fits me like glove. There are elements I do identify with. The intense ambition for getting on, which is something that I have only lately come to realise I have myself. (Frank 1994)

Asked if she liked the character, Mirren replied:

> Yes and no. I enjoy disliking her. She isn't always a nice person, she can be selfish and driven. Those aspects are actually quite attractive in that they are forceful and dramatic. We're accustomed to seeing neurotic or hysterical women characters – victims – but we rarely see a woman whose faults are directly related to her strengths. The only way to change the perception that women have to be consistently perfect is to show that we're not. (Hayward and Rennert 1996: 15)

At other times she has said: 'I think the fact she could be unlikable is one of the reasons she was popular ... sometimes being a female character is a bit like being a black character ... You can't be selfish and greedy unless you're like Joan Collins in *Dynasty*. You can't be an ordinary flawed person' (Frank 1994). The point Mirren is making here is that whereas white male actors have the freedom to play a wide range of character types, women and black actors are limited to a much narrower range of roles because of the ways in which gender and ethnicity are socially constructed. Mirren's achievement was to create a character who was 'political without being propagandist', who 'inspired some women to be more confident and optimistic' (Hayward and Rennert 1996: 15). In her foregrounding of emotional affect, she extended the possibilities for female characterisation and career-orientated protagonists in traditionally 'masculine' professions, such as Professor Sam Ryan (Amanda Burton) in *Silent Witness*, as well as opening the door for more psychologically orientated crime dramas such as *Cracker*.

The four mini-series (1991, 1992, 1993, 1996) and the three two-hour dramas (1995) that constitute the on-going series of *Prime Suspect* were watched by more than fourteen million people on each occasion. The programme has sold in more than fifty-two countries worldwide and has made Mirren an international star. As the series developed Mirren scooped a number of best actress awards and became a national celebrity, renowned for her sexuality as well as her acting skills. Her public image subtly changed as the media paid more attention to her physical appearance and her glamorous 'older woman' persona. In the popular press, there was a shift away from discussion of her acting skills to articles that addressed female readers through a focus on the problems faced by professional women in the workplace, frequently offering 'off the peg' solutions concerned with dress, makeup and how to deal with issues such as sexual harassment. The typical magazine 'makeover' of the professional woman offers hints on how to achieve the Mirren 'look' if you're a busy working woman; in the *Daily Mail*, for example, under the heading 'A Fair Cop', Mirren is described as tough but elegant, wearing 'leading Italian label MaxMara for the majority of her wardrobe in the award-winning television drama' (Rolfe 1993). On 10 April 1994, she featured in a *Sunday Times* article, 'The State of Glamazonia', on Britain's most glamorous women, and in an article on how to 'power dress' containing advice from management consultants and psychologists to other successful professional women 'who like DC Jane Tennison ... often [have to] sacrifice their femininity' (Turner 1994). There are numerous interviews and articles with women in traditionally male occupations and a series of articles on women in the police force ranging from accounts of sexual harassment cases ('Where bigotry is part of the job; a policewoman tells of her victory over racial and sexual abuse' (Bedell 1993)) to the *Sun*'s report on the work of a 'real' DCI headed 'I hate Helen Mirren, I'm just a woman trying to catch a killer' (quoted by Campbell 1995). On the appointment of a woman to the rank of chief superintendent the *Daily Record* ran 'Super Sandra; or Superintendent to you Constable' (Clarke 1995) and the declaration made by the newly appointed Chief Constable of Lancashire Police Force Mrs Pauline Clare that 'I've never felt a need to become one of the boys' was reported in *The Times* (Alderson 1995). These articles present Mirren as a touchstone for working women who want to succeed in a man's world; in all of them Mirren is the generator of an equal opportunities discourse around the (hetero)sexual desirability of older women and their professional abilities, building on the image of the 'new woman' of the 1990s.

This flurry of interest in the older working woman can be interpreted as an acknowledgement of the role that mature women are required to play in maintaining modern capitalist societies. Rosalind Coward (1978) argues that popular discourses work constantly to redefine women's sexuality in relation to the shifting demands of capitalism for labour by constructing new areas as sensual and equating that sensuality with work (quoted by Baehr 1980a: 31). Within this context, this particular version of the 'new woman' is a reinscription of the post-war discourse that constructs professional women as women who sacrifice their personal lives to serve society and its public institutions as a consumer-orientated discourse that recognises the potential spending power of the older woman and her value as earner, customer and consumer. The sponsorship of the *Prime Suspect* series by the car manufacturing company Peugeot to the tune of £250,000 only serves to underline the point; they used the advertising space to promote the new Peugeot 106 as an exciting car for women drivers. It was not, however, the older woman viewer who was 'having it all' or even the series creator La Plante, but the production company Granada; they increased their advertising revenue and income from programme sales due to the series' high ratings and critical claim, a financial coup not lost on La Plante.

Mirren's image replaces outmoded post-war depictions of mature professional women as authoritarian matriarchs, eccentric spinsters and 'blue stocking' intellectuals. By presenting her as a desirable and sexually attractive woman off-screen, publicity and promotion of Mirren reinstates the sexual quotient that is missing on-screen, left out perhaps because of the ITC's rulings on taste and decency. In *The Times* Mirren is described by Alan Frank as:

the driving, untouchably sexy, some would say ruthless, maler than male policeperson at the core of this most realistic of television series ... much of the power she commands as Jane, both as boss and object of desire, derives from the certainty that the animal attraction is presently ... hemmed in by a combination of decorum, rank and uniform. (Frank 1994).

'Exploding' Tennison's image in this way situates the female public servant, the formerly prim and respectable woman of duty, as someone who has sexual desires and needs. Although her image is contained within conventional notions of femininity, it confounds expectations of the spinster, the dominant image of the dutiful woman in post-war western culture, the asexual woman who 'sacrifices' her personal life to serve the 'greater' good (of religion, the nation, the state) and the dominant status quo. In contrast to an earlier generation of film and television dramas that depicted professional or career-orientated women as sacrificial and reforming characters, *Prime Suspect* portrays Tennison as demanding the opportunity to practise her skills, to be acknowledged for her professionalism and to have a sexual identity. Unlike many contemporary images of professional women in traditionally male occupations and various forms of public service that depict women as compromising their femininity by transgressing traditional boundaries of gender difference (for example, Dr Kerry Weaver in the US series *ER* (NBC 1994–) embodies the distorting force of female ambition in her physical appearance and actions), Tennison functions as a fully realised, psychologically complex character in the public sphere even if her private life remains in disarray.

   This is a considerable shift in generic conceptions of the relationship between women and professional identity, where the depiction of 'backstage' emotional behaviours that humanise male professionals serves only to undermine the credibility of professional women (Hallam 1998; Philips 2000). For some critics, however, Tennison's failure in her personal life, her inability to form lasting relationships and her non-motherhood ultimately undermine her success. In Eaton's eyes, for example, the depiction of Tennison as a 'failure' on the personal front serves to reinforce doubts about her validity as a woman (Eaton 1995: 175). La Plante herself is very clear about why she decided to focus on Tennison's professional rather than her personal life:

> One of the reasons why I walked away from *Prime Suspect* was that they wanted to focus on her private life, whereas the reason why I wrote Jane Tennison was because she's a woman who's won her position on merit by climbing up through the ranks. My long-term aim was to take her to being Chief Constable, like Alison Halford. There are plenty of writers focusing on women's sex lives. I choose not to. (Allen 1998)

Once La Plante left the series, Mirren became involved in producing ideas and shaping the development of the character. Sally Head, Granada's controller of drama in the early 1990s, believes that Granada still managed to maintain a 'special atmosphere' that allowed creative people space to exercise their initiative in spite of changes at senior management level within the company and the new system of central-ised scheduling organised by the independent television network. The three two-hour dramas in 1995 were based on ideas Mirren discussed with Sally Head: 'I thought it was time for a change. One four hour story is very difficult to produce and I was frightened of not being able to get another really good script. I thought it would be interesting to change it into two-hour stories, which is classic film length' (Hayward and Rennert 1996: 14). Mirren and Head also thought that the two-hour format would make the drama easier to sell in the international market. In retrospect, Mirren considers that the characters suffered as a result; there was far too much emphasis on plot at the expense of the kind of attention to psychological detail that makes Tennison such a compelling character. Setting *Prime Suspect 5* in Manchester was also Mirren's idea; the city 'has a powerful personality and character of its own, visually and physiologically' (Hayward and Rennert 1996: 13). The integrity of the series continued to be maintained, at least in part, because numerous people on the production team have provided continuity through the different productions: 'I associate my character so much with those people that the moment I see them I fall straight back into the role' (Hayward and Rennert 1996: 14). Here, Mirren points to the collective, ensemble nature of TV drama production and the continuity provided by the television studio production system, a continuity that Thomas Schatz (1988) called 'the genius of the system' in his analysis of genre films produced in the heyday of the Hollywood studio system in the 1930s and 1940s. Working with the same people can create a team ethos of excellence that overrules the notion that any one person, whether writer, director or star, is the single 'author' of a film or TV drama.

Mirren's own position as the leading character in *Prime Suspect* has shifted over the years towards greater assimilation between the actor and the role, a shift that has altered her star persona from the sex symbol of the art cinema and renowned stage actress to mainstream glamour icon and television celebrity. At the same time, like La Plante she has been caught in the tide moving television drama away from its theatrical heritage towards a more commercial emphasis on genre and the star appeal of leading actors. Stars, as Richard Dyer (1979) has argued, serve a double function in society; they are both sites of erotic desire and socially symbolic signifying systems, 'signs of their times' that circulate in a range of media texts, their meanings changing historically. Film stars are one of the earliest forms of contemporary celebrity, their mass-marketed images promoted by studio marketing campaigns and the gossip press epitomised at the beginning of the second millennium by magazines such as *Hello* and *Heat*. Contemporary press and magazine features and articles on Mirren bear all the hallmarks of 'celebrity biography', timed to coincide with the release of her latest work, another series of *Prime Suspect*. Celebrity biography also characterises the ways in which La Plante talks about her work in pre-broadcast press releases. P. David Marshall argues that this intense focus on the public individual is a peculiarly modern phenomenon that effortlessly celebrates democratic capitalism (Marshall 1997: 4). In this sense, La Plante's 'strategic penetration' of the crime genre and her subsequent financial success can be viewed as a rather different form of intervention than that envisaged by Trevor Griffiths in his attempt to disrupt the conventional naturalism of television drama in the 1970s or that envisaged by feminist critics concerned with identifying the 'progressive' potential (or not) of certain kinds of texts.

La Plante, understandably perhaps, has a rather different view of authorship based on her experience of *Prime Suspect*'s runaway success; as the awards for the series mounted up and the international sales rocketed, she became Britain's best-known television writer. Taking the cue from other successful creative women such as Madonna, she decided to take control of her work. Rather than writing successful series for corporate companies she decided to start her own production company and 'strategically penetrate' the nexus of vested financial interests that constitutes the male-dominated film and television industry. The following chapter charts her success as an independent producer who has to make money to survive in the business and traces the effects of her financial and business strategies on the development of her work.

Notes

1 *Prime Suspect 6* Granada/WGBH Boston co-production in association with CBC, executive producer Andy Harris, produced by David Boulter, written by Peter Berry, directed by Tom Hooper. Note that there are no longer any women involved in the key creative and/or institutional positions. The executive producer of the first series was Sally Head.
2 Jenny Sheridan became deputy controller of network drama at ITV in November 1993.
3 For accounts of these interventions see, for example, Hallam and Marshment (1995), Carson (2000) and Tylee (2000).

4 The name is a reference to a 1980s American political scandal centred on election rigging dubbed 'Watergate'.

5 BAFTA placed *GBH* and *Prime Suspect* in the serial drama category; at the RTS awards, *Prime Suspect* won in the best single drama category, indicating a degree of confusion between the definitions; see Powell (1992).

6 Peter Kilfoyle (2000) offers an account of the local government conflict in Liverpool during these years.

7 Exceptions are 'nostalgic' crime dramas in which the female investigator is modelled on the Christie prototype, such as *Hetty Wainthrop Investigates* (BBC 1990–9), a Patricia Routledge vehicle, and the adaptation of P. D. James's *An Unsuitable Job for a Woman* (ITV 1997) starring Helen Baxendale and Annette Crosbie. Both are set in small towns rather than urban areas and rely on typically 'feminine' attributes such as gossip and intuition as well as personal observation to solve local mysteries.

8 Emile Zola formulated a theory of fictional representation in which he proposed that the writer should study men and women as the naturalist studies animals; 'naturalism' demanded comprehensive and meticulous description of the material world as well as of characters and their situations. See Hallam with Marshment 2000: 5.

9 Tasker (1998: 115–37) provides a detailed analysis of these shifts in relation to *film noir* and new Hollywood, quoting a *Daily Mirror* review of *Body Heat* in which the love scenes are 'couplings of extraordinary eroticism which a few years ago would have had the censor reaching for his scissors' (22 January 1982).

10 Following the Broadcasting Act of 1990, responsibility for monitoring taste and decency shifted from the Independent Broadcasting Association (IBA) to the Independent Television Commission (ITC). In 2003/4, the role of the ITC was absorbed by the new telecommunications and broadcast regulator Offcom.

11 The McPherson report enquired into the failure of the Metropolitan Police to convict the murderers of Stephen Lawrence, a nineteen-year-old black man killed in a racist attack. It reported in 1999, some six years after the crime was committed.

12 'Operation Care' was launched by Merseyside Police in 1997 after allegations of widespread and systematic abuse of young people housed in local authority care homes during the 1970s and 1980s. Similar investigations took place in a number of other local authority homes throughout England and Wales.

13 For a detailed analysis of professionalism as a male construct and the implications for female professionals and professions see Davies 1996.

14 I have reserved the term 'naturalism' to refer to its literary antecedents in Zola and Naturalist philosophy, but the term is imprecise and is often used to refer to Method-trained actors. I have argued elsewhere that 'realism' is more accurate term in this context: see Hallam with Marshment 2000: 3–23.

15 Thornham's analysis is based on material in the listings magazines 30 November –6 December 1991.

Lynda goes to Hollywood

4

The popular and critical success of *Prime Suspect* enabled La Plante to launch her own production company and become engaged in a range of new projects, including developing a screenplay. This final chapter examines the first phase of her career as a writer/producer in the UK and her initial forays as an independent producer into the highly competitive US film and TV marketplace. Encouraged by the success of *Prime Suspect*, UK drama commissioners dusted off La Plante scripts sitting on their shelves and put them into production. In the four years between *Prime Suspect* in 1991 and La Plante's first independent production venture with Verity Lambert in 1995 a total of eight dramas written or devised by La Plante were broadcast, ranging from the two-part four-hour film format of *Comics* (C4 1993) to *The Lifeboat* (BBC 1 1994), a six-part series devised and part written by La Plante. These 'quality popular' dramas are indicative of changing priorities amongst drama commissioners as they chase high ratings, marking a shift in production culture away from the public-service ethos of British television culture towards a consumer-orientated, market-driven model. Tackling controversial subjects based on contemporary issues, La Plante's dramas proved popular, creating fertile ground for critical debate in the press and attracting high ratings.

The first section of this chapter offers a brief summary of these works before focusing on two of the first independently produced dramas to develop earlier themes of strong women through a focus on independent female characters: *She's Out*, the final series in the *Widows* trilogy that La Plante co-produced with Verity Lambert's company Cinema Verity, and her first stand-alone project, *The Governor*. The second section examines the period between 1995 and 1997, when La Plante made her first film for US television, *The Prosecutors* (NBC 1996) and a more formally experimental series for ITV, *Trial and Retribution* (1997). A harrowing story of the murder of a young child based on close observation of police practice and legal procedures, *Trial and Retri-bution* was seen by a number of critics as 'too complex' for ordinary television viewers because of its split-screen format. The series was created with an awareness of the changing ways in which people watch and engage with television through various forms of advertising, youth programming and web design which rely on viewers selecting information from a number of competing images and graphics on the screen. Arguably La Plante's split-screen innovation – a technique later used to critical acclaim by Mike Figgis in his feature film *Timecode* (2000) and further developed in the highly regarded 'real time' American drama *24* (US/BBC 2001–) places La Plante in the vanguard of developments in television drama.[1] Her ability to integrate experi-mental techniques within generic formats makes her one of the few contemporary British crime dramatists who can reconcile the conflicting demands of commercial production for more of the same kind of 'safe' programming with hard-hitting contemporary themes wrapped in innovative formats.

Prime Suspect 3 was a critical hit in America as well as in Britain, winning an Emmy for best mini-series. La Plante identifies this as the moment when she decided she no longer wanted to be 'just a writer for hire':

> The real brick to the head – it seems petty now to say this – was when Granada Television informed me that the Emmy Award for *Prime Suspect* belonged not to me but to the producer. I thought of all the time I'd spent in Aids clinics, all that time with the police, to get that story and then the producer hired a crew and filmed it! I didn't own it, I was just for hire. (Lawson 1998: 87)

Perhaps the way in which she was passed over by Granada and Uni-versal Studios in favour of scriptwriter Tom Topor in their negotiations to make the first *Prime Suspect* into a £12 million movie also played a part in her decision to start her own independent production company, although the film failed to materialise (Evans 1992). Shown in America early in 1992 as a weekly three-part serial in the PBS *Mystery* slot, *Prime Suspect* was widely popular and critically acclaimed as a 'Brittanic *Hill Street Blues*' because of its emphasis on equal opportunities issues (Scott 1992). *Prime Suspect 2*, presented in the same slot a year later, was greeted with muted enthusiasm; *Prime Suspect 3*, screened in 1993, was considered a return to form, securing La Plante's reputation as a writer of 'quality popular' drama in the US. Reviewed in *Variety* before it was transmitted in Britain, the series was praised for David Drury's atmospheric direction and La Plante's excellent script, while Helen

Mirren's performance enshrined DCI Jane Tennison as 'one of the great female characters to emerge from British drama' (Elley 1993: 57).

Following *Prime Suspect 3* La Plante attempted to capitalise on her success by forming her own company and setting out to seduce the American market, a common dream amongst successful UK television writers but one that very few achieve. Her friend and former colleague Verity Lambert, by this time running her own independent production company, provided the role model and practical guidance that enabled La Plante to take creative and financial control of her work, while producer Steve Lanning taught her the realities of raising finance and controlling the budget for *The Governor* (Allen 1998).

Creative and commercial contexts: BBC and ITV drama production

> I couldn't go to Hollywood – they're all such wankers, and with television I've got everything I need. (La Plante in Grant 1992: 20)

La Plante's emergence as a significant drama writer cannot be severed from the industrial context in which she works. Following the popular and critical success of *Prime Suspect* La Plante became one of the most sought-after writers of the early 1990s. Her ability to raise serious issues within popular formats was regarded by commercial broadcasting executives as a guaranteed solution to the problem of meeting contending demands for 'quality', made by the regulators in the wake of the Broadcasting Bill, and for the kind of profitability that is achieved by selling audiences to advertisers. The BBC was also attracted to the kinds of drama La Plante was writing, but for slightly different reasons. Following the passing of the Broadcasting Act in 1990 attention shifted from re-regulating the commercial sector to the recurring issue of funding the BBC; once again the licence fee was placed under the spotlight of government scrutiny. With its charter due for renewal in 1996 and renewed speculation about its future, the BBC was keen to demonstrate that it provided 'quality' programmes that were good value for money, that it could continue to attract a large proportion of the diminishing terrestrial audience share and that it met criteria for equal opportunities across its production slate. The commissioning of Jeanette Winterson's controversial lesbian coming-of-age drama *Oranges Are Not the Only Fruit* (BBC 2 1990) is a typical example of this shift in policy as the BBC sought to capture the 'marginal' audience served by Channel 4 (Hallam and Marshment 1995).

The requirement of the Broadcasting Bill that all terrestrial broadcasters commission 25 per cent of their total broadcasting output from independent production companies broke the monopoly on in-house production that dominated the British TV system. The government's policies aimed to make the programme market more competitive as well as creating more opportunities for diversity among programme makers; in practice, this meant that broadcasters shed permanent staff as they downsized their companies to remain competitive, or, in the case of the BBC, cost effective. Production became separated from transmission, a situation exacerbated within the BBC by the development of internal cost-accounting measures that introduced an internal market and a system known as 'producer choice' whereby producers were encouraged to seek the cheapest means of programme-making available in an attempt to make the BBC's in-house facilities commercially competitive. Launched in 1991, the intention of 'producer choice' was to reshape the BBC's internal management structures in order to equip it for the objectives spelt out in its campaigning document *Extending Choice in the Digital Age* (BBC 1992).

One effect of these measures was that many skilled production staff left the BBC to set themselves up as independent producers and/or freelancers. Drama production was particularly hard hit by these changes, with the result that whole departments closed down, pushing up the costs of in-house production as under-used departments struggled to remain financially viable (Berkeley 2003: 111). The Broadcasting Bill also changed the ITV drama commissioning process; an Independent Television Network Centre was established to centralise decision-making within the ITV system with the aim of making Channel 4 more competitive.[2] Inevitably, smaller ITV companies found it difficult to survive in the fiercely competitive atmosphere; changes in rules regulating media ownership in 1996 saw large companies such as Granada and Carlton buying smaller companies and, in a parallel wave of accumulation and consolidation, large independent producers buying out their smaller competitors. Critics of this process argue that decreasing numbers of corporate owners do not compete with each other to produce quality programmes; they compete to produce programmes that will deliver audiences to advertisers. The result is a proliferation of cheap, formulaic products that are similar rather than different as terrestrial broadcasters continue to try and corner their 'market share' of the diminishing audience (see, for example, Curran and Seaton 2003). The diet of programming available in the mid-1990s confirmed these fears as cheap-to-produce 'makeover' and reality TV shows percolated through the day-time schedules into prime-time mid-evening slots while terrestrial broadcasters demonstrated a continuing reliance on popular drama such as soap opera, crime series and medical melodramas to deliver high audience ratings.

In this climate of change and uncertainty, safe generic products were given high production values and increased sexual and violent content to attract and entertain more affluent viewers; critics concerned about taste and decency in television programming became alarmed about the increase in sexual and violent content in prime-time dramas. 'Quality' drama, one of most expensive forms of television product to produce, continued to be made but was increasingly considered a flagship product, indicative of a broadcaster's national and international status and restricted to 'safe' generic productions that sell in the international programme marketplace, such as crime dramas and 'heritage' adaptations of well-known literary classics. The spiralling price of 'quality' drama production demanded that costs were recouped through international co-production funding partnerships with other independent producers and national broadcasters to spread the risk of investment and secure guaranteed distribution deals.

Following the merger of Rupert Murdock's Sky and the UK consortium British Satellite Broadcasting in 1990 the terrestrial broadcasters had to face up to the realities of growing competition from satellite. For two years following the merger in 1990, BSkyB lost money; subscribers grew steadily from 1.77 million households in 1991 to 3.56 million households by mid-1996. In 1992 the company started to make a profit, estimated by 1996 as an annual turnover in excess of £311 million (Syfet, quoted in Goodwin 1998: 53). At least two trends in programme production were discerned as a consequence of the increased channel choice offered by BSkyB, both of which are arguably a consequence of demographic shifts in the gender and age of terrestrial-channel viewers. The first cable and satellite subscription channels to sell were sport and movie channel packages, both favoured by affluent younger male viewers and, in particular, the wealthy twenty-five- to thirty-year-old ABC sector highly sought by advertisers. These were followed by popular youth-orientated music channels and children's cartoon channels. This led to a degree of 'feminising' of the four terrestrial channels, apparent in the growing number of magazine-style 'makeover' and cookery shows in the 8.00–9.00 p.m. prime-time evening slot and an increase in the kinds of generic drama that would engage female viewers (Brunsdon 2000: 169). More female writers were commissioned, their different worldview providing fresh themes and an innovative point of view for stale generic formats that attracted high numbers of terrestrial viewers as well as fulfilling potentially conflicting demands for quality drama and equal opportunity. Writers such as Lucy Gannon and Kay Mellor proved that they could create engagingly plausible worlds orientated around women and their points of view that attracted high ratings; these are not necessarily 'feminist' dramas but they tackle contemporary issues of importance to women and are informed by feminist commentary and debate, perhaps fulfilling the criteria of 'post-feminist' dramas, although the term is subject to ongoing contestation and debate (see, for example, Brunsdon 1997 and Hollows 2000: 190–204).

With women breaking through the glass ceiling in a range of traditionally male occupations and taking their place in the workforce on an apparently equal footing with men, the media proclaimed the mid-1990s a 'post-feminist' era; women had won their battle for equality and the issue was no longer sufficiently interesting or newsworthy. Within the media industries, however, such claims were undoubtedly premature. In television women were far more visible on the screen as newscasters, investigative journalists, hosting quiz shows and playing leading roles in drama but investigations of women's work behind the screen continued to reveal that much of this was superficial 'window' dressing. *Her Point of View* (1993), a report commissioned by the Women's Broadcasting Committee on Women in Television and BECTU, concluded that the BBC was more likely to screen work with women as producers and directors, that Channel 4 was least likely to screen work with women as producers or writers and that ITV screened the most work by women writers but had the lowest proportion of women directors and editors; overall women were thinnest on the ground in drama, light entertainment, arts and sports programmes, more common in documentary/current affairs, schools and children's TV. The British Film Institute's tracking study of women's careers in television provides an interesting snapshot of changing employment practices in the industry and how these impacted on female work patterns during the decade. By the mid-1990s the industry had changed from employing predominantly salaried staff on unlimited contracts to a workforce composed of more than 60 per cent freelancers working on short-term contracts (Skillset estimate 1996, quoted by Willis and Dex 2003: 121). As terrestrial broadcasters divested themselves of 'surplus' production staff in order to meet new financial targets, programming was increasingly supplied by numerous small and a few large independent producers, a trend that grew apace towards the end of the decade. These companies tend to employ freelancers on short-term contracts; with no clear career structures, networking and personal contacts become important ways of finding out about available work opportunities. In what many consider is still an aggressively 'macho' working environment with impossible production schedules and long hours of work, women taking 'time out' to have a baby or devote attention to their family risk losing essential contacts as well as their confidence (Willis and Dex 2003: 128–9). The BFI's research revealed that the workforce looks more equal in terms of gender distribution in the younger age groups and that some women are achieving top positions but most of these women are childless; equality of opportunity has come about by worsening men's conditions of work and creating a climate that is intolerant of responsibilities outside of the television workplace (Willis and Dex 2003: 139).

La Plante has commented on these conditions in interviews on a number of occasions, saying that if she had been fortunate enough to have children she would not have pursued her career in the same single-minded way. 'There is no doubt if I'd had a family, I wouldn't have done any of this' (Iley 1992). Since running her own production company she has also become more aware of sexism and sexual discrimination in the television industry and the critical establishment, claiming that 'I've become too successful for the (pseudo-intellectual) male hierarchy to tolerate', which she says was not the case when she was 'just a writer for hire' (Glover 1996: 16). It seems that women in the UK television industry who seek financial parity with their male colleagues, similarly to female producers and writer/producers in the US, continue to face discriminatory practices because of their gender, and that in spite of huge inroads made by women television is still a male-dominated sphere in which women have to become 'one of the boys' in order to compete on equal terms with men (Alley and Brown 2001).

The progress of La Plante's scripts through the terrestrial broadcasting system in the early to mid-1990s provides a microcosmic case study of changes in the industry at this time. Quick to realise that her dramas guaranteed high ratings, television executives brushed the dust off scripts languishing on their shelves and rushed them into production. *Civvies*, a six-part serial that La Plante began to work on following *Widows*, waited four years until Ruth Caleb was given the green light to produce it for BBC 1 in September 1992. *Seconds Out*, a BBC/Granada co-production, was completed for the autumn 1992 *Screen One* portmanteau slot on BBC 2. *Framed*, a two × two-hour mini-series made by Anglia Television, was shown later the same year on ITV. *Seekers*, a two × two-hour mini-series produced by Lawson Productions for Central Television, was broadcast early in 1993 on ITV. *Comics*, a two × two-hour mini-series, was commissioned by Channel 4 from Lambert's company Cinema Verity and screened in 1993. *The Lifeboat*, a series devised and part written by La Plante for Bloom Street Productions, aired on BBC 1 in 1994. It is worth noting that all of these dramas apart from *Seconds Out* and *Framed* were produced by women, lending substance to arguments voiced by industry activists in the 1970s that more women producers would lead to more commissions for female writers. Unexpectedly perhaps, given La Plante's pioneering exploration and development of leading roles for older women, five of the dramas are centred around male protagonists; only *Seekers*, based on two female private investigators (played by Brenda Fricker and Josette Simon), continued to explore familiar themes of women and detection. *Seekers* was initially developed for US television in the mid-1980s but was dropped because of La Plante's insistence on a black female character bearing the child of a white man; 'I wouldn't alter her, so it ended up being shown here' (Gritten 1993: 40). The series focuses on what many UK critics regarded at the time as an implausible premise: the relationship between two women who share a husband, only to discover that he is a bigamist after his death. Together, they establish and run a private detective agency while mutual respect for each other blossoms into love.

Other dramas of this era explore issues of violence and homosocial bonding that characterise male institutions and environments: *Seconds Out* centres on a young boxer who is framed for rape by an unscrupulous manager and pushed into the unlawful sport of unlicensed boxing; *Comics* delves into a world familiar to La Plante from her acting days, that of the stand-up comedian touring the comedy club circuit; *Framed* focuses on an unlikely character, a supergrass, played by former James Bond actor Timothy Dalton. The most controversial of all these dramas was undoubtedly *Civvies*, a story about ex-paratroopers returning to civilian life after serving in the armed forces. Widely acknowledged to be one of the most graphic depictions of violence in a television drama at the time, the series was defended by La Plante as an attempt to raise public awareness of the effects of post-traumatic shock, a condition the army refused to accept as a medical condition needing treatment. La Plante claims she wanted to make public the army's position on this occupational hazard; at this time they provided no general training or support for stress-related problems and disorders and no system of aftercare for sufferers (Collins 1992). According to La Plante, intensive research for the series revealed that employers are reticent about giving jobs to ex-paratroopers, not least because their rigorous training makes them too institutionalised and unable to think for themselves. The characters in *Civvies* are based on a group of ex-soldiers that La Plante says she met when building work was carried out on her house shortly after the Falklands War between Britain and Argentina over sovereignty of the Falkland Islands. She listened to their stories and paid them for their time. Insisting that the events, particularly those set in Northern Ireland, are based on facts, she wanted the drama to be a wake-up call to the plight of young men sent to the province as 'peacekeepers', to make people more aware of the long-term psychological effects of violence on British soldiers. Noting an increase in the superficial news coverage of celebrities and their lifestyles in the national daily newspapers, La Plante claims she sought to re-engage public interest in the deaths and injuries sustained by young men in the ongoing war.

Civvies is focused on the de-mob experiences of ex-staff sergeant Frank Dillon (Jason Isaacs) and five of his former squaddies who have difficulty readjusting to civilian life after some twenty years in the army, not least because of the problems they face finding work. Unable to support their families, they seek refuge from feelings of uselessness and low self-esteem in alcohol and drugs, quickly leading to family breakdown. Acts of extreme violence are a learnt response to any threatening situation; the men's aggressive outbursts on civvy street are interspersed with numerous flashbacks to their days of active service in Northern Ireland, a graphic means of depicting the psychological damage resulting from surviving violent and life-threatening situations. The series depicts loyalty amongst men in the most taxing of circumstances; a pub bombing has left one of Dillon's men, Steve (Peter Howitt), severely injured with a permanent tube in his throat that needs vigilant attention to prevent suffocation. Dillon himself suffers from vivid flashbacks of the traumatic events that left him and his fellow soldiers dead, maimed and psychologically scarred. Themes of male bonding and affection are explored in some depth, with tender scenes of caring, particularly between Frank Dillon and the suicidal Steve, that, like the relationship between Shefford and Otley in *Prime Suspect*, border on the homoerotic.

Civvies was not viewing for the faint-hearted and elicited numerous complaints, including a severe reprimand from the head of the parachute regiment. Before the series was broadcast, commanding officer Lieutenant General Sir Michael Gray wrote to the BBC to complain about the series' 'numerous inaccuracies', 'objectionable' story and the portrayal of soldiers as 'maladjusted misfits'. The BBC responded by asserting that the drama was fictional, not a factual programme: 'We are not making a PR film for the Army' (Summers 1992: 15). After watching the series Gray withdrew his complaint, admitting that it offered a plausible depiction of post-army life.

Civvies was greeted enthusiastically by one female critic as 'quintessential La Plante: macho, violent, every line as tough as if it was written by a long-term male recidivist who had taken a literary course behind bars' (Summers 1992); it seems probable that Summers was thinking here of men such as Jimmy Boyle, the convicted Glaswegian murderer who published his autobiography in 1977. Male critics were less enthusiastic and accused La Plante of depicting maleness as a disease, of creating violent, drunken, moronic characters who are deeply sentimental and resentful of anyone with power. Interestingly, such critics label La Plante's writing as 'commitment TV', suggesting that the kind of issues she tackles in her dramas could have been undertaken in the previous decade by crusading current affairs programmes such as the long-running *World in Action* or *This Week*, both of which became casualties of ratings-driven competition in the early 1990s (Paterson 1992a, 1992b, Jefferies 1992). La Plante vigorously defended herself against these attacks, claiming that as a writer she doesn't shun male violence, she aims to get inside it: 'People accuse me of only giving my full attention to villains or fighters, and in a way I think that's true' (Summers 1992: 15).

In these dramas, there was less emphasis on female characters; women in *Civvies*, for example, were kept in the background, leading to accusations that La Plante had written a weak part for Dillon's wife. La Plante publicly refuted these criticisms, claiming that 'they missed the point, she's the real survivor, she keeps the family together, she goes out to work and does well ... she's not weak, she's strong' (Grant 1992: 20). Throughout the early 1990s La Plante's most successful dramas offer a female point of view in a man's world or put forward a critical view of male behaviour. In this sense La Plante is sometimes regarded by journalists as a feminist – a label she firmly ignores – because she offers a judgmental perspective on male behaviour rather than because she projects positive representations of women or tackles women-centred issues and topics.

Commercial incentives: La Plante Productions

> These days a television writer needs to know the market like a book-maker. (Lawson 1998: 86)

It is possible to discern three clear tendencies developing in La Plante's work by the mid-1990s. One of these has its roots in and a commitment to the traditional concerns of the single play and the 'realism of record'. Social issues are presented in a sociologically realist style that emphasises psychological realism and authenticity of characters, situations and settings; examples include series such as *Civvies*, the film drama *Seconds Out* and *Comics*. The second strand integrates social issues and realism within traditional generic formats. Crime dramas such as *Prime Suspect* and the first *Trial and Retribution* mini-series integrate socio-logical realism with generic realism to provide one definition of how the crime series helped to determine the development of 'quality popular' television in Britain in the 1990s. An alternative definition is provided by the third strand of La Plante's work, which abandons sociological realism altogether in favour of intertextuality and the highly wrought emotional landscape of glossy prime-time melodrama. Here high pro-duction values, musical underscore and contrived plots create a form of drama more readily associated with popular American formats where the focus is on individual tragedy and personal circumstances rather than socially extended commentary. Two British dramas of the mid-1990s, *She's Out* and *The Governor*, as well as providing inspiration for the spectacular production values and convoluted plot structures of later series and serial melodramas such as *Bad Girls* (ITV 1999–) and *Footballers' Wives* (ITV 2002–), bridge the gap between the earlier issue-based drama that characterises La Plante's most critically acclaimed work in Britain and her move into the territory of prime-time melo-drama exemplified in her second work for American network television, the mini-series *Bella Mafia*.

  She's Out (Carlton 1995) is a return to the familiar territory of female-centred drama developed in *Widows* with key members of the original cast and production team reprising their roles; Ann Mitchell returns as Dolly Rawlins, Ian Toynton as director and Verity Lambert as the pro-ducer. Reminded by a fan that Dolly, convicted of murder after shooting her husband at the end of *Widows 2*, was due to be released from prison in 1995, La Plante decided to write a follow-up series once she had sorted out the contractual obligations with Disney, who by this time owned the rights to *Widows*.[3] La Plante was able to purchase the rights to bring back one character, Dolly, but had to construct a scenario without on-screen reference to any of the other key characters; hence the focus on ex-prisoners who meet Dolly on the inside, 'very, very tough women', characters not often seen on television in leading roles. In an interview for the *Independent*, La Plante explained, 'I'm attempting to write six hours of television dominated by women. No love interest, nothing else, but I also didn't want to make a piece of "feminist" pro-paganda, something strident' (Benedict 1994: 25). The result is a melo-drama centred on Dolly and six ex-cons who hope to get their hands on a share of the diamonds hidden at the end of *Widows 2*. Newly released from prison, Dolly is invited to a welcome party by former prostitute's madam Ester (Linda Marlowe) at her crumbling mansion in the country-side, an erstwhile 'health' farm. When Dolly discovers that Shirley's mother, left in trust of the diamonds, has sold them for a fraction of their worth to buy a villa in Spain, she decides that the only way she can fulfil her cherished ambition to turn the run-down mansion into a children's home is to persuade her companions to hold up the mail train, a robbery planned and executed with La Plante's characteristic attention to strategic details and technical precision.

Part of the pleasure of *She's Out* is that of generic anticipation. The crumbling mansion invites speculation: will there be a murder to solve? Will the house be haunted? There are elements of both in a drama that unashamedly raids the generic wardrobe to dress a story of greed and revenge with vestiges of the western and the gothic crime thriller. After a rather slow start to the first episode that offers a long exposition of Dolly's chastened circumstances since the last series of *Widows 2,* the series gathers momentum as the motivations of the motley crew gathered to 'welcome' Dolly become more apparent. Dolly becomes embroiled in a battle of wills for the support and control of the 'gang' as she plans a daring mail-train robbery on horseback. There are slight parallels in the narrative, suggested in a brief opening shot of the women on horseback brandishing shotguns, with the story of *The Magnificent Seven* (Sturges 1960) where a group of reformed gunslingers are persuaded to become the protectors of the community. Here, however, only Dolly has altruistic aims. Unlike their western antecedents, most of these women are born to be bad; they put aside personal differences to undertake the great train robbery, but are ultimately destroyed by their inability to trust each other. The audacious plot culminates in a spectacular action sequence; for most of the last episode it looks as if, yet again, Dolly has pulled off the job, but ultimately she is undone by Ester's jealousy and suspicion. Unlike in La Plante's earlier dramas, there are no graphic images of horrific violence and there is certainly no attempt to be either politically or morally correct.

Although there were more leading roles for women by the mid-1990s, most of them were for young women; openings for older women outside the ghettos of soap opera and comedy were still few and far between.[4] Mitchell, aged fifty-five by 1995, had few television roles following her success in *Widows*; she continued her stage career, winning awards for her performance in the title role of *Hecuba at the Gate*, taught drama at London Guildhall University and ran drama workshops at Holloway Prison, an excellent preparation for reprising her role as Dolly. Once again, La Plante's series was welcomed in the press for the 'strong and meaty lead roles written for women' (Francis 1995: 20). For the most part however critics disliked the series, commenting on its excessiveness and lack of plausibility: 'the train hijack on horseback was particularly hilarious' (Hildred 1995: 15). With an audience of more than eleven million people television executives were happy in spite of the critical disdain; once again a La Plante drama had delivered the coveted prime-time audience. Part of the attraction for viewers was perhaps the diversity of the women, their range of backgrounds and their disastrous relationships, a failing marriage and a lesbian love triangle providing the only source of romantic interest. Each of the women was an emotionally damaged but talented character demonstrating skills and abilities such as Gloria's confident knowledge of guns and how to use them, Julia's riding skills and Connie's ability to seduce men. Like Dolly, their characters combined toughness with tenderness in various measures, but it is Dolly who emerges as the strongest character, her determination to provide a home for unwanted children the motor that drives her criminal endeavours and her final demise.

The struggles between the women have class and sexual undertones. Ester and her girlfriend Julia are middle-class women whose relationship is founded on the financial value and use of each other rather than affection, warmth or sexual desire. Julia, a former doctor, is a recovering drug addict; Ester, a former prostitutes' 'madam', is a wily manipulator and heavily in debt. The other women are working-class and do as they are told, though not without grumbling. Dolly's clash with Ester can be read as a class conflict in which Dolly's abilities and her professionalism contend with Ester's belief that she is better than the others and therefore has a right to order people around and run the show. Ester's insistence that she knows best has no basis in her skills or abilities when it comes to planning robberies, which is why Dolly is able to challenge her authority. The depictions of lesbian identity are somewhat contrived in service of the plot. Ester's only feeling for Julia seems to be jealousy, while Julia uses her ability to sexually attract women to manipulate them; her affair with a local policewoman, driven initially by mutual desire, becomes a way of gaining the policewoman's confidence in order to access her home and find out about her movements.

With their exaggerated traits and plot functionality, the characters are typical of those that traditionally furnish melodramatic landscapes. Ester is a (failed) arch villain amongst thieves, Dolly a heroic defender of the weak and innocent, a veritable Robin Hood. The train robbery is a spectacularly realised melodramatic set piece, excessive not only in the extravagant use of special effects, but also in the conception of its staging. The subplot is convoluted and overly dependent on coincidences. Dolly helps a young woman who, unknown to her, has had an affair with the dead Shirley's brother, now a crooked detective and a member of the team at a local police station. She reveals what she knows of

Dolly's plans to him, but Dolly's meticulous planning and attention to detail enable the women to stay one step ahead of the police by concealing all traces of their involvement. Ester's lack of trust in her partners in crime creates a final twist in the plot that is completely unexpected. After the robbery, the police visit the house to talk to Dolly about the licence for the children's home; Ester, unable to believe that Dolly is not betraying her, shoots her in cold blood. With Dolly's death, the plot finally achieves closure and the *Widows* trilogy is complete.

With its exaggerated characters, plot contrivances, use of coincidence and spectacular climax, *She's Out* bears all the hallmarks of nineteenth-century stage melodrama and classic silent movie comic heists such as *The General* (1926) repackaged for contemporary consumption.[5] For her next female-centred drama, La Plante returned to the theme of a woman breaching the boundaries of a traditionally male profession, this time combining sociological realism and 'commitment' drama with a more melodramatic style. *The Governor* is the first drama to be solely produced by La Plante Productions; the idea for the series developed while La Plante was researching *Civvies* and regularly visiting prisons. During these visits she met Alison Gomme, at that time thirty-two years old and the only female governor of a high-security male prison in England. Gomme asked La Plante to write her story; La Plante obliged, writing a two-hour pilot as an introduction for a subsequent one-hour weekly series (White 1995: 41).

The structure of the pilot episode shares some similarities with the first *Prime Suspect*, including a double narrative that is the story of both governor Helen Hewitt's attempt to discover the truth behind a suspicious death in the prison and an investigation of professional malpractice that reveals overt misogyny and homophobia among the prison officers. Hewitt (Janet McTeer) is placed in charge of a male prison following a serious riot in which an inmate serving a life sentence for paedophilia and child murder is found dead; although the circumstances of the death are suspicious, the prison staff claim the prisoner committed suicide. The men in Hewitt's charge are convicted of violent sex crimes, sadistic murders and arson – men who could have been arrested and convicted by DCI Tennison. Like Tennison, Hewitt discovers and has to deal with endemic corruption amongst her staff; the prison officers' systems of incentives for good behaviour are corrupted by bribery for favours, creating an incendiary situation between prisoners and officers that Hewitt, as governor, has to manage and contain.

Comparisons between Tennison and Hewitt reveal an interesting addition to La Plante's repertoire of professional femininities. If Tennison is the avenging angel who seeks retribution and punishment for crimes committed against women, Hewitt is the ministering angel who believes in the power of forgiveness and redemption. On one level, Hewitt's role in *The Governor* depicts a form of authoritarian matriarchy associated for much of the twentieth century with the image of the hospital matron; like the matron Hewitt runs a total institution and is responsible for the care and control of staff and inmates alike. She shares with her nursing sisters a degree of idealism and self-sacrifice; there is an air of the salvationist about her, an image sustained in part by her appearance, her long blonde hair and long skirts accentuating the 'angel' analogy. Like the stereotypical professional nurse she is a woman with a mission, driven in this case to reform and redeem the murderers and thugs in her care, although her powers are tightly constrained by Home Office civil servants and a male-dominated board of governors. Disliked by the rank and file prison officers and abused by the hierarchy, who seek a scapegoat for the mismanagement that led to the rioting and the suspected murder of an inmate, Hewitt receives emotional support only from her former boss and mentor, a female governor of a women's prison. Like Tennison, Hewitt is an isolated, childless figure, a divorced woman now married to her job in what can only be described as an emotionally abusive relationship, but the image she projects, softened by her appearance and an unassertive but determined demeanour untainted by 'masculine' traits such as swearing, is a more traditionally feminine image than that projected by Tennison.

The emphasis on Hewitt's femininity opens up a credibility gap between the character and the role she has to perform. She has to assert her authority against frighteningly violent adversaries who use a barrage of crude sexual insults aimed at embarrassing and humiliating her in front of other inmates and prison staff, scenes strongly reminiscent of Clarice Starling's treatment when she enters the criminal asylum in *The Silence of the Lambs*. Throughout these encounters Hewitt stands her ground and looks her chief adversaries in the eye, her unwavering gaze silently returning their hostile stares as they pour forth torrents of verbal obscenities. The experience literally sickens her; to relieve her extreme tension she vomits in the privacy of the toilet. Such filling in of the character's 'backstage' behaviour humanises Hewitt, but showing 'feminine' weakness in this way is equally problematic as the depiction of Tennison's more aggressive 'masculine' behaviour in *Prime Suspect*. Hewitt's performance of professional femininity plays to stereotypical depictions of women that project them as emotionally weaker than men. When a male character in a position of authority is shown as a caring, emotional individual it serves to humanise his character rather than diminish his authority; in female characters such behavioural responses only serve to reinforce social constructions of gender that depict women as 'the weaker' or 'the gentle' sex, ruled by their emotions and unable to conduct themselves in a suitably disinterested and dispassionate manner (Hallam 1998). There is, of course, no solution to this problem of representation within the signifying constraints of popular drama; culturally, images of women are overloaded with social and symbolic significance that ascribe them polarised identities as melodramatic embodiments of culturally prescribed traits (Macdonald 1995). It is these aspects of female representation that La Plante explores further in her first two productions for American network television, *The Prosecutors* (1996) and *Bella Mafia* (1997).

Crossing the pond

> Jane Tennison stormed onto the American television landscape in January 1992 ... she was as mad as hell and wasn't in a mood to be ignored – not by her superiors at the Southampton Row police station and certainly not by millions of viewers who immediately realized they were watching something new and unique, not only for *Mystery!*, but also for the whole television medium. (Miller 1996: 95)

In spite of her protestations in 1992 that writing for television offered her everything she might need, following the success of *Prime Suspect* on US television La Plante began to court American television and film executives in the hope of securing the lucrative deals that would grant her executive producer control over her own work. She was no stranger to the Hollywood film and television scene; Thames had attempted to sell the format of *Widows* for American network syndication in the mid-1980s and Granada the film rights for *Prime Suspect*, an experience that led her to vow only to write drama for television. Perhaps her marriage to an American helped La Plante bridge the cultural gap between British and American writing and production styles that is often considered the reason why British films and TV series only achieve limited success in the American market.

For whatever reasons (and they deserve more consideration than I offer here), La Plante has been more successful in selling her ideas to US media executives than any British television writer before her. Her first commission was to create a legal drama; the result was *The Prosecutors* (NBC 1996) starring Stockard Channing as the aggressive smoking and drinking wheelchair-bound lawyer Ingrid Maynard – a veritable female Ironside![6] In style and appearance, the two-hour tele-film is similar to many other American made-for-TV movies of the mid-

1990s, echoing elements of the form and structure of the 'true story' film that centres on the biographical experiences of a living individual to strengthen its claim to authenticity, although in this particular case there is a disclaimer to the effect that all the characters and events depicted are fictional. The double plot structure of *The Prosecutors* focuses on two female lawyers who work for the district attorney, one of whom is rising to the peak of her career, the other an appeals expert whose high-flying career has been curtailed by a road accident leaving her without the use of her legs. Commonly in this type of telefilm, a story of personal tragedy and overcoming adverse circumstances is used to make a rhetorical case for an unpopular or minority viewpoint (Hallam with Marshment 2000: 110–14). In this case Maynard is depicted as a victim of her own hubris, bitterness and self-pity as well as of the social marginalisation that results from her physical impairment.

An interesting aspect of this drama is its early attempt to engage with issues of virtual violence against women on the Internet, a theme that La Plante returns to in her British drama *Killer Net* (1997). When District Attorney Rachel Simone (Michelle Forbes) is faced with a personal tragedy, she asks Maynard to take over a test case in legal protection for women, that of prosecuting a man for unlawful harassment on the Net. Whereas Simone is prepared to fight the case on the basis of ethical argument, Maynard sets out to find evidence of the accused's Internet activity, which includes uncovering other instances of harassment. Maynard wins the case and with her confidence restored returns to her pre-accident status as a trial lawyer. This time, her inability to stand up in court to defend her client is insufficient reason for the district attorney's office to prevent her from practising; the legal system has to overcome its prejudices and accommodate her.

The Prosecutors is made in a slick fashion that seems typical of American telefilms; it has high production values, a named star and two writers in addition to La Plante. Visually, it is shot in a cold colour range characteristic of American police and legal series, with blues, greys and blacks predominating, but it is not a *neo-noir* imitation; the focus on the two lawyers also makes it distinct from earlier ensemble legal dramas such as *L.A. Law* (20th Century Fox Televisioin/NBC 1986–94). The two women represent different ethical positions and different inter-pretations of their professional role. Simone relies on arguing the case on a basis of moral principles, fairness and mutual respect, an 'ethics of care'. Maynard is more concerned with providing arguments supported by hard evidence to fight her case, an 'ethics of justice' (for a more detailed account of these distinctions, see Gilligan 1993). The former is presented as a more 'feminine' position, embodied in Simone's presentation of self as a grieving wife and mother. Maynard, on the other hand, looks uncared for and neglected, in an attempt at what Jane Feuer describes as 'uglification'; Feuer argues that the stars of made-for-TV problem movies 'consciously uglify themselves' to emphasise that they are 'real people' (Feuer 1995: 22). Channing's attempts to realise her character are reliably predictable; Maynard smokes, drinks, swears a lot and is abrupt and aggressive, all characteristics associated with masculine behaviour. Her methods of legal practice are evidence rather than theory based, placing her in a generic tradition of male television investigators stretching back at least as far as the 1960s when Raymond Burr played the wheelchair-bound detective Robert Ironside.

In 1997 La Plante's own adaptation of her 1990 novel *Bella Mafia* was broadcast in the US as a four-hour mini-series. Vanessa Redgrave starred as Graziella Luciano, the respected wife of a Mafia don with four sons, the eldest of whom, Michael (Michael Hayden), is murdered on the eve of leaving Sicily to attend law college in America. Nastassja Kinksi plays Michael's lover Sophia and Jennifer Tilley a showgirl who marries one of the Luciano's younger sons. Stripped of the sociological commentary and claims to authenticity that are hallmarks of La Plante's British crime dramas, *Bella Mafia* expands the melodramatic territory developed in *Widows 2* and *She's Out* by adopting the high production values, glossy appearance and highly wrought emotional atmosphere typical of prime-time US melodramas such as *Dallas* (1978–91) and *Dynasty* (1981–91) in their later years. An operatic story of murder and violent revenge, the star-studded mini-series was nicknamed a 'lasagne opus' by the *Variety* critic in recognition of its homage to Coppola's *Godfather* trilogy.[7] The plot hinges on a series of unlikely coincidences focused on the reappearance of Sophia's illegitimate son Luka (James Marsden), who was sired by Michael before his impromptu demise. Sophia has married one of Michael's younger brothers and has two young children. Luka, unaware that Sophia is his mother, kills all the male members of the Luciano family, including Sophia's children, in act of vengeance on behalf of his adopted father, a sworn enemy of the Lucianos who, unbeknown to Luka, murdered his father Michael before he was born. Hiding his identity, Luka becomes a suitor to one of the bereaved Luciano women while flirting outrageously with the others until Sophia realises that he is not who he claims to be but her long-lost son. To avenge the deaths of her legitimate children and her family, Sophia cold-bloodedly kills Luka and takes over the family business, becoming a veritable Godmother.

The first two hours offer the nostalgic pleasures of historical costume drama and a rural setting, with convincing performances from the cast.

Following the assassination of the oldest son Michael, the slow pace of
the drama offers ample opportunity to enjoy the spectacle of landscape
and performance during a lengthy expositional sequence until the action
quickens in the second half as the characters, in age-old tragic fashion,
hasten to meet their preordained destinies. The killing of the children is
graphically depicted as a cold-blooded and brutal act; one by one they are
muffled with their pillows and shot. With all the male members of their
family killed, the grieving women find that they have between them the
determination and skills to take control of the family business, including the strength to kill others in defence of their property and status.
Values of care and co-operation amongst the women combine with 'post-
feminist' attributes of business acumen and 'masculine' emotional
detachment to create an image of wronged women for the 1990s that
reiterates and reinforces mythic and symbolic images of wronged women
in western culture as furious avengers and defenders of their young.

Bella Mafia established La Plante as a screenwriter/producer of some
significance in America; a high-budget production with major stars, it
was deemed 'quality' drama in the US press because of its attention to
style and appearance. The plot, however, stretches the patience of any
viewer interested in credibility. In this it seems to echo the implausible
happenings of 1980s prime-time soap operas such as Dallas and Dynasty,
their screening in Britain and subsequent popularity regarded by many
British critics as the beginning of a decline in the public-service values
and 'quality' of British television (see, for example, Ansorge 1997). The
response to Bella Mafia from the British press was, predictably, less
than kind: Adam Sweeting in the Guardian commented, 'If La Plante
had hired a committee of D-list hacks to cobble together a version of
Widows acceptable to American TV, it would have looked like this'
(Sweeting 1998).

Trial and Retribution

> Many television dramatists are frustrated stage or movie writers. La
> Plante, you feel, wants to be in the box, and brilliantly knows how to fill
> it. (Lawson 2000: 17)

Amidst her forays into the US film and television scene, La Plante
continued to write dramas for British television. Trial and Retribution
(1996) is her third contribution to the crime series and her most
formally experimental and innovative, marking a return to sociologically
committed drama and a renewed interest in the genre. Once again La
Plante introduces new generic content, redressing a representational

gap in her *oeuvre* by following a crime from its inception through the search for evidence to the arrest and conviction of the accused, effectively filling in the gaps in narrative detail left out between *Prime Suspect* and *The Governor*. Psychological profiling of the key suspect introduced in the first *Prime Suspect* is extended to include an examination of the emotional fallout of the crime on those touched most deeply by it, the victim's close relatives and the policeman who finds the body of the murdered child.

Screened on ITV in two parts on two consecutive nights in October 1997, the four-hour mini-series centres on the search for a five-year-old girl from the moments just before her disappearance until the week following the trial when forensic evidence confirms the guilt of the prime suspect, already found guilty of the child's murder by the jury on the basis of circumstantial evidence. The series is a return to the familiar ground of police procedure and the painstaking attention to accurate and authentic detail that mark La Plante's most critically acclaimed work to date. The cast of characters includes the family of the missing child Julie Ann Harris (Millie Ricks), the detective in charge of the search for her DI Pat North (Kate Buffery), her boss Detective Superintendent Walker (David Hayman), the young policeman who finds the body (Jake Wood), the prime suspect Michael Dunn (Rhys Ifans), his female lawyer (Anastasia Hille) and a number of witnesses in key supporting roles. The harrowing story examines the psychological impact of Julie's abduction and murder on her mother Anita (Helen McCrory), her young brother Jason (Mitchell Ray) and her mother's live-in boyfriend Peter James (Lee Ross). The collapse of PC Barrage following his discovery of the body and the denial of the crime by the disturbed young man who is finally found guilty of the child's murder add to the emotionally charged atmosphere.

La Plante's emphasis on the detailed depiction of police procedures and practices reveals the fallibility and difficulties of detective work while never allowing the viewer to forget the ethical complexities of attributing blame for the murder and bringing the accused to trial. In this mini-series, following a number of controversial cases of miscarriage of justice which resulted in the wrongful imprisonment of suspects, La Plante touches on a growing mood of concern in UK society about the administration of justice as she reveals the imperfections and moral frailty of a system controlled by political expediency and financial exigency. Through detailed depiction of interaction between the police and the Home Office's legal administrators, the political and financial pressures on police investigative work become apparent. The Crown Prosecution Service and the legal profession are shown to control decisions about the amounts of time and money that can be spent on collecting the evidence for any one case and the basis on which a suspect can be brought to trial. The lawyers are Machiavellian manipulators who serve their own interests; their analysis includes an assessment of the evidence as well as decisions about the conduct of the trial, a control that appears to promote the financial interests and professional status of the lawyers at the expense of the victims and their families. The police are relatively powerless, well-intentioned but flawed public servants who have to work within frameworks determined by strict financial limitations and shifting political priorities and considerations.

The accused, Michael Dunn, is in many ways a predictable suspect; an abused child himself without parents or family, brought up in a series of care and foster homes, he lives a life of alcohol-induced oblivion and chronic self-abuse. Convinced by circumstantial evidence that he is the killer, the jury finds him guilty. Helpless against the machinations of the law-and-order machine, he seems a sacrifice to social prejudice until, in the final sequence, forensic tests confirm his guilt some days subsequent to the trial. Until that moment, it is possible to believe, as his lawyer does, that Dunn is innocent, a victim of circumstances. The ending is far from comfortable; it remains conceivable that Julie Ann's stepfather Peter, revealed as a child abuser during the police investigation, is the perpetrator of the crime in spite of belated forensic evidence that confirms Dunn's guilt. In a harrowing final sequence, Dunn raves and screams in his cell, 'I didn't do it, I didn't do it', creating a disturbing sense of doubt rather than the comfortable reassurance that usually accompanies closure, regarded as a hallmark of the genre.

The unsettling experience of viewing *Trial and Retribution* is increased in part by the way that the story is told using split-screen narration, in part by Evelyn Glennie's unobtrusive award-winning soundtrack, which maintains a low-key presence throughout.[8] In most detective series the linear progression of the plot tells the story of the piecing together of another story, that of the crime; here that structure is defamiliarised through intermittent use of a split screen that offers multiple viewpoints on the action, destabilising the authority invested in the detective's gaze as the person who controls what is known, which in turn disturbs and undermines the comfortable position of superior knowledge usually afforded the viewer in crime series. The tripartite screen interrupts the chain of narrative causality, switching attention to juxtaposed close-ups, replays and multiple viewpoints of situations and events, calling into question the truth of what is seen and what is said and revealing the complex memory lapses and motivations that form the nexus of the investigation.

Initially the split screen is used to accentuate the claustrophobic environment in which Julie Ann is growing up, an East End of London characterised by high-rise living, loneliness and alienation, a world away from the comfortable familiarity of the fictional world of community depicted in BBC 1's *Eastenders*. The opening sequence emphasises the grimness of the locality, an urban prison of high-rise flats seen through barbed-wire fencing, the hard angles of the rectangular pillars and concrete balconies dissecting the frame to emphasise the physical and psychological entrapment of living in an environment ravaged by poverty, unemployment and crime. Three juxtaposed images depict five-year-old Julie and her brother Jason in the children's playground, a fenced area in front of one of the housing blocks. Julie is shot through the wire, trapped behind the fence in a grey environment drained of colour against which her blonde hair and red jacket innocently stand out as she plays beside the peeling paintwork of a once brightly painted roundabout. Some viewers, mindful of the intertextuality of much contemporary television and film, may associate the blonde-haired child and her red jacket with an earlier story of the tragic death of child in the psychological horror film *Don't Look Now* (Roeg UK/Italy 1972). The simple bell-like tones of the soundtrack emphasise feelings of foreboding, a ghost track of memory that calls to mind a children's song, simultaneously drawing attention to the game of peek-a-boo Julie is playing with an unseen person who reaches out and leads her away by the hand. She disappears from view watched by the only witness, elderly Mrs Marsh, who can see the roundabout from her balcony as she waits for her meals on wheels lunch to be delivered.

In the sequences that follow the simple musical theme is replaced by an ominous low chord as Anita and Peter begin a frantic search for their missing child. Once Julie Ann is reported missing to the police, the action switches from the family to the police team. As the search intensifies and continues into the rain-swept night the sense of apprehension that the child will not be found alive is accentuated by stylistic references to contemporary *neo-noir* films, such as eerie blue lighting and the disquieting tones of a muted low chord on the soundtrack. In these sequences, the split screen is used to depict the scale and intensity of the search for the missing child; rather than cross-cutting between scenes, parallel activities are juxtaposed to create a dense visual texture. The screen is split into three or four sections, each of which depicts a different aspect of the search, creating a heightened sense of tension and immediacy; long shots of policemen searching and close-ups of what they see and the clues that they miss are presented side by side. This juxtapositioning and parallelism effectively extend the impression of time, drawing out the search and creating a heightened sense of realism, of witnessing the process of searching – for evidence, for the child, for the truth.

La Plante's reinvigorated use of realist conventions in *Trial and Retribution* complements the development of reality TV police programmes that show edited camcorder footage of real-time video recordings of police work such as *Blues and Twos* (ITV 1993) and *Police Camera Action* (ITV 1995), shunning the action-driven sensationalism of drama series such as *Thieftakers* (ITV 1995–7) in favour of meticulous attention to the procedural processes that finally results in charging the suspect and bringing him to trial. There are no fast-cut edits across the segmented multiple narrative characteristic of many popular series and serials, no spectacularly edited sequences of chase and arrest; heroes, villains and action all play a secondary role to the slow exposition of procedure and process. The split-screen technique increases the psychological intensity of the drama by emphasising a number of competing truths, any one of which could be *the* truth since all accounts are shown to be partial versions of events pieced together from shards of evidence and fragments of memory.

The final sequences of the series are focused on the court room and it is here that the split screen is used to its greatest effect, intensifying psychological and narrative tension as the events around the time of the murder are slowly pieced back together. In most detective series, the story of the investigation unveils the story of the murder; here, the process of detection has yielded clues and amassed circumstantial evidence but it is the process of the trial itself that pieces the jigsaw together. It is an incomplete picture; no one saw what happened, nobody's gaze is privileged as *the* gaze, neither police nor lawyers occupy a position of superior knowledge and nor does the viewer. Absolute certainty of the killer's identity is obscured from view: no one admits to killing Julie Ann, no one witnessed who abducted her. Until the forensic evidence confirms Michael Dunn's guilt, identifying his fingerprints and the child's blood on a broken bottle, responsibility for the murder can only be established by the accumulated weight of circumstantial evidence, a situation which bears unhappy correlation to real-life circumstances that is far from reassuring as closure.

Peter James's potential guilt is kept in play throughout *Trial and Retribution*; with their long hair, long coats and scruffy clothes, he and Dunn are superficially alike and could easily be misidentified by witnesses. Peter is not the father of the children and has a criminal history of violence; both Julie Ann and her brother Jason have bruises on their bodies that point to violent physical abuse at home. Anita too begins to have doubts about Peter's innocence when he insists that she corroborates his version of events around the time of Julie Ann's disappearance. Suspicions that Peter may be the killer continue during the course of the trial; here the split-screen technique is used to remind viewers what people claim to have witnessed by juxtaposing flashbacks of former accounts and parallel events as the lawyers sum up the case in their final addresses to the jury. As the case is made against Dunn, one image depicts Jason leaving his home with a social worker; Peter has persuaded Anita to place him in care, his rejection and dismissal of the child a reminder that he may have played a part in Julie Ann's violent death. Another image depicts a further casualty of the crime, PC Barrage handing back his uniform and his police badge, his psychological health irreparably damaged by the disturbing experience of finding the dead child's body. Earlier images of the small bruised and battered body crushed in the drainpipe and then cradled in Barrage's arms counterposed with images of Julie alive and laughing in the playground and her puffy lifeless face are the most disturbing images in the drama; Barrage's distress embodies that disturbance, his rational self overwhelmed by feelings of helplessness and rage. Determined to avenge the child's death, he manufactures evidence against Dunn, but unable to bear the burden of his own guilt, he breaks down and admits culpability.

Throughout the trial the split screen keeps alive these different narrative threads. Testimony is sometimes accompanied by simultaneous actions elsewhere, sometimes a reminder of counterfactual information offered by other witnesses. This complex narration seemingly allows viewers access to the psychological process of solving the crime; it offers a privileged position of knowledge from which it is possible to weigh up the circumstantial evidence, assess known facts and judge their accuracy and validity, placing the viewer in a similar position to that of a member of the jury. In the attempt to wrest clues from the physical and emotional responses of witnesses and suspects, to forge certainty from surface appearances, to dispel all reasonable doubt, it becomes obvious that forensic science offers the only secure ground on which such judgements can be based. Here, the radical form of *Trial and Retribution* stands in contrast to its more conservative treatment of theme; generic renewal serves to reinstate the credibility of policing by a focus on police practice that reveals the authority invested in the Crown Prosecution Service and the machinations of the lawyers who run the system.

Split-screen narration avoids the need to cross-cut continually between parallel story sequences, maintaining a sustained focus on events without sacrificing contemporary demands for faster-paced delivery of story information to the shorter sequences and rapid cutting techniques termed by Robin Nelson 'flexi-narrative' (1997: 24–5).[9] The most significant aspect of this method in terms of the police series, and the way in which La Plante develops it in subsequent series of *Trial and Retribution*, is the use of a slow but relentless narrative pace counterpointed by close-up, parallelism and repetition. This replaces the action-driven narratives of earlier police series with a psychological mode of storytelling that emphasises how difficult it is to 'know' the mind of an 'other', to discover motivations, isolate causal factors. Whereas soap opera is sometimes credited with enhancing viewers' ability to read emotional responses to situations because of a tendency to focus on the characters' emotions through close-ups of their faces, in La Plante's police series the intense study of the suspect's emotional response provided by extreme close-up has the opposite effect. The difficulty of 'knowing' a person by reading their facial responses is manifest during intense sessions in the interview room and the witness box where the use of extreme close-up increases narrative tension; extreme close-ups dissect the face, reducing it to a series of fractured and fragmented features, indicating the interviewer's difficulty in decoding a potential suspect's reactions. The feeling created by the final sequence, with its tight close-up on Dunn's distorted face, is one of relief because uncertainty is over – the suspect is guilty as charged, the system can 'deliver' – but not one of reassurance. As the maniacal Dunn raves and screams from his cell, 'I didn't do it, I didn't do it', it is still possible to think that he might be an innocent victim of the machinations of the legal system, a distinctly uncomfortable conclusion.

Commenting on trends in UK police series during the 1990s and their relationship to what she terms 'the structures of feeling' in society at that time, Charlotte Brunsdon (1998: 242) argues that the genre raises questions about 'Who can police?' and 'Who is responsible?' In the *Prime Suspect* series La Plante addresses these questions through the liberal solution of an equal opportunities discourse; in *Trial and Retribution*, she shifts the terms away from scrutinising those who police to those who are responsible for ensuring that, as a society, we have laws that work and the people and resources to ensure they are administered justly and fairly. La Plante's drama asks 'How do we know who is guilty?' and 'Whom can we trust to judge?', questions that this mini-series leaves unanswered, perhaps reflecting a growing unease in British society with outdated systems of public administration and a loss of faith in a legal profession designed to ensure that all people in society have equal rights to justice and are treated fairly by the law. The inability of a misogynistic, homophobic and racist police force to solve crimes effectively that was manifest in *Prime Suspect* has shifted to a critique of the outdated practices of the criminal justice system and the role of the legal profession, its class-based and status-bound behaviours made particularly apparent in Dunn's conversations with his lawyer, in which he mocks her use of terms such as 'plank' to describe the prosecution witness. Sexism as well as class difference is ingrained in the system; returning from a prison visit to see Dunn, Belinda's fellow lawyers talk about her perfume and mock her 'female smell', making indirect reference to the sequence in *Silence of the Lambs* where Clarice Starling has to endure convicted murderers and rapists making insulting comments about her body odour. The tenor of the remarks made here by professional men who act like overgrown schoolboys is more polite but the implications of the insult are similar. Even so, it is hard to feel empathy for the self-righteous Belinda, who labours under the twin burdens of status consciousness and professional snobbery. Without paying due regard to the evidence against her client or thoroughly probing his alibi, she is convinced he is innocent merely because the solicitor she works for has little regard for the Crown prosecutor and has appointed a respected and successful defence barrister to take the case.

In contrast, the police are depicted as capable professionals trying to solve problems in difficult circumstances. Pat North is a competent organiser, less concerned with fighting her (male) colleagues then Jane Tennison and more at ease in her work – perhaps a measure of the ground gained in the fictional world of the crime series where being a woman in charge of an investigation is no longer regarded as the exception rather than the rule. DS Walker (David Hayman) and his team, brought in to investigate the murder, are reminded by North on more than one occasion of the facts and details of the case; Walker, a cop of the old school, has the grace to acknowledge her contribution, his patronising attitude thrown into sharp relief by North's refusal to rise to the bait. It is North who finally cracks the case following a conversation with a key female witness who reveals facts to her that she has not discussed in court. Earlier themes of gender and policing explored in *Prime Suspect* are integrated here into a narrative that tackles wider concerns about systemic problems of accountability within the institutions of the criminal justice system. There is a stronger sense in *Trial and Retribution* of the relationship between characters as active agents and the wider institutional structures they have to work within than in La Plante's previous work. North works at the local level, Walker at district management level; both are subject to the dictates of the Home Office and the Crown Prosecution Service. By locating the characters within these institutional structures, the series refuses the generic trend away from public experience and recognisable realities in favour of the dramatic licence granted to formulaic action-based products noted by Sparks (1992) or the nostalgic pastoral offered by other 1990s police series such as *Inspector Morse* and *Heartbeat*.

Because the police officers/agents work within a framework which is critical of institutional structures, *Trial and Retribution* is a candidate for what Nelson terms 'critical realism'. Nelson argues that critical realist TV drama, unlike formulaic generic drama, offers the resources for criticising dominant institutions and the status quo by providing additional perspectives with potential to open up new ways of seeing, broadening viewers' horizons and loosening their conservative ties with the world (Nelson 1997: 230). The first series of *Trial and Retribution*, with its harrowing portrayal of parental loss and exposure of fallibility in the legal system refracted through the focalising apparatus of split-screen narration, offers a different way of experiencing the crime series and its relationship to the world of external realities. The series met a mixed reception; before it was broadcast critics claimed that it would confuse viewers, who would find it difficult, if not impossible, to read three or four different images at once on a domestic television screen. La Plante argued that such comments underestimate the audience, who are accustomed to reading advertisements and TV news bulletins, both of which are frequently more visually complex than her tripartite screen structure (Francis 1997: 18). Following the broadcast of *Trial and Retribution* the critical reception was rather muted, although there was a predictable debate about the increasing use in ratings-conscious television drama of harrowing images intended to shock viewers. The *TV Times* invited viewers to contact them with their reactions to the images of the child's dead body in an article that argued that BBC dramas are equally determined to shock viewers as their commercial counterparts such as *This Life* (BBC 1995–), depicting explicit sex, and *Holding On* (BBC 1997) featuring a brutal stabbing of a young woman in a phone booth. A report by the Broadcasting Standards Council revealed that 62 per cent of the viewers they polled considered that there was too much violence on television; other dramas condemned for offensive scenes included Jimmy McGovern's *Cracker*, Kay Mellor's *Band of Gold*, *The Governor* and *Silent Witness* as well as imported US dramas such as *The X Files* and *Millennium*. Liz Jarvis, deputy features editor of the *Radio Times*, added her own comment: 'Violent images in TV drama can only be justified if they're essential to the continuity of the plot. Anything else is just gratuitous' (Power 1997: 20).

The depiction of violence and the use of images of dead and mutilated women has created unease in many quarters. La Plante's interest in serial killing, forensic science and realistic portrayal of corpses, considered ground-breaking in the first *Prime Suspect*, is manifest in many of her productions. *Trial and Retribution 2* (ITV 1998) explores these themes in explicitly graphic detail. The spectacle of women's breasts hacked from their victims and images of their mutilated dead bodies created a flood of complaints to the Broadcasting Standards Council and renewed accusations that La Plante favours sensationalist spectacle rather than psychological exploration of characters, that her dramas are vehicles for the pornography of violence masquerading as entertainment. Peter Patterson of the *Daily Mail* was particularly vociferous, asking 'who took the decision to unload this bucket of filth on a Sunday, the biggest viewing night of the week, when most of us would have been expecting just another cop drama?' (Paterson 1998a: 55). La Plante was equally strident in her own defence against such accusations, but this time the complaints to the Broadcasting Standards Council were upheld; Yorkshire Television were roundly admonished for broadcasting images of gratuitous violence. Perhaps because of these criticisms, later series of *Trial and Retribution* are less centred on the detail of forensic work and more focused on the activities of the police. The split-screen format loses some of its interrogative power, becoming more of a device for paralleling the action of a number of 'flexi-narrative' plot strands rather than a way of questioning different versions of the 'truth'. The first two series of *Trial and Retribution* currently stand as La Plante's last efforts to integrate 'the realism of record' into the melodramatic format and generic realism of the crime thriller. In later series, the police, the villains and the structure of the plots are more predictable, marking the transition to 'blockbuster' dramas focused on melodrama and spectacle that becomes prevalent in La Plante's work by the end of the decade.

An unsuitable job for a woman?

By the late 1990s, La Plante's reputation in the Britain was changing; she was no longer heralded as a writer of compelling, controversial dramas with a strong social message but was accused of using moralising messages as a means to depict explicit sexual scenes and gratuitous violence against women. Her work was charged with being tired and derivative, produced with one intention only, to make money. It is interesting to consider whether her gender is a factor in this outburst of critical derision; after all, Alfred Hitchcock, a maker of genre films featuring countless murders, serial killers and sophisticated acts of physical and psychological violence against women, is now regarded as one of Britain's greatest filmmakers, his body of work examined in numerous studies that attempt to find reasons for his endless fascination with the killers and their victims. Dennis Potter, deemed Britain's most talented and productive writer of television drama, also produced fantasies that were misogynistic and debasing of women without receiving the flood of critical condemnation heaped on La Plante's later productions. Dubbed by some critics 'TV's Mr Sex', Potter was granted artistic licence to pursue his projects in his own way; his pornographic imagination was attributed to childhood experiences and tended to enhance rather than detract from his overall reputation as a writer dealing with serious themes and issues (Pearson 1995: 1). La Plante's ongoing engagement with themes of sexual sadism, murder, serial killing and forensic science is evident in her novels as well as in her crime dramas and melodramas. Could it be that the subject matter of the television crime series, although explored by numerous female writers in crime novels, is still deemed 'unsuitable' territory for a woman creating drama for mainstream audiences, particularly when it emphasises entertainment values rather than issues of social concern?

La Plante has always resisted any simplistic correspondence between her life experiences and the characters she creates, although critics are often keen to attempt to make a connection. Many of her 'strong' women are single, childless women, for example, who have progressed in their careers because they are without a long-term partner or dependants. Responding to questions about the relationship between her life experiences and her work, La Plante is always ready to admit that there might be a little bit of her in her characters, but states that the inspiration for them is based on external factors, on people that she has met, stories she has been told, people she has interviewed with the intention of using the research to construct a composite character, taking details from one aspect of a person and putting them with another until the character takes on an identity and personal characteristics that will serve the purposes of telling the story. When asked about how she writes, La Plante sometimes comments that she bases all her work on research because that is the only way she knows how to write, she does not have a university education, she is not trained in academic or literary ways of thinking and writing. There is always a defensive tone in her response to these questions and, more recently, more than a hint of anger at the ways in which she is judged by what she terms 'the pseudo-intellectual hierarchy' of professional television criticism in the UK.

That such a barrier can exist between a writer and her critics is perhaps due to the hierarchies of taste that continue to linger in the British literary and cultural establishment and the ways in which these inform and shape attitudes to television. Television occupies a marginal position in the humanities curriculum – perhaps, as Sue Thornham has cogently argued, because of its complicity with mass culture and the feminine (2003: 75–94). It is notable, in this context, that the form of drama that is television's most abiding contribution to our culture, soap opera, is also the one that until its rehabilitation by feminist critics received the least critical esteem. Labelled a 'feminine' form of drama because of its appeal to the female audience, its endlessly repetitive scenarios of family life are seen to be in tune with the distracted concentration of women viewers, themselves preoccupied with the daily minutiae of family routine (Modleski 1982); or, as John Fiske (1987) has argued, the cyclical rhythms of the drama seem to embody the repetitive reproductive cycle that determines biological female sexuality. Within this context, authorship is often used as a term to signify the 'quality' of individually written works rather than team-written series and serials such as soaps, to indicate those dramas that are written especially for television rather than adapted from novels or screenplays (Day-Lewis 1998).

Critical condemnation of La Plante's work was widespread by 1998, provoking questions about why a writer who self-consciously admits that she writes for profit received such vicious treatment in the press. Evaluation of a writer's work is always, by definition, a retrospective exercise, often undertaken posthumously or at least once the author has reached sufficient maturity and level of output to warrant in-depth critical attention. Evaluation within authorial traditions of criticism is invariably based on constructing a person as a creator of great talent and distinction whose works make their mark by being judged as whole or truthful in relation to the human condition. In television drama, the definition of the writer as an author with a unique vision has been applied primarily to those working within the single-play tradition, with Dennis Potter's work often held up as the standard against which all else is measured (Hallam 2000b). Acclaimed writers of 'quality popular' drama such as Lynda La Plante and Jimmy McGovern who make their mark in generic forms such as crime thrillers cannot be claimed for authorship status in quite the same way as their predecessors writing for the single-play slot in earlier decades, not least because the very nature of genre fiction is that it is a commoditised form of artistic production against which authorship is always defined.

The critical history of television drama begins with an authorial approach vested in traditions of analysis drawn from literature and the stage. Nelson (2001: 8) offers a succinct analysis of the ways in which TV drama has been evaluated and studied, initially through a focus on literary and writer-centred credit given to the playwright (e.g. Brandt 1981). In this conception of the role of the critic, the audience benefits by the critic's interpretation of insights into 'the human condition' which are inscribed in the text and made available to the discerning reader. Subsequently more theoretical debate has reflected the dominance of 1970s 'screen theory' with its privileging of textual form and notions of Brechtian distanciation. Proponents argue that anti-realist strategies enable viewers to adopt an intellectual, thinking approach to television rather than being 'co-opted' by becoming emotionally engaged by the characters and, through their agency, into the dominant ideology, a view that Nelson suggests might be more suited to analysing avant-garde cinema than popular television texts. Commenting on these approaches, Nelson notes that although they are quite different in their political affiliations, 'it is perhaps ironic that both "screen theory" (coming from a Marxian left) and Brandt (coming from a centrist liberal position) invite academic interpretations of the scriptures to be passed down where a stable significance is allegedly fixed and transparent' (Nelson 2001: 8). Authorial critics such as Brandt celebrate the liberal tradition of the single play as the form that permits public airing of contemporary (and sometimes contentious) issues through the distinctive expression of an author licensed to voice his (sic) opinion.

Critics such as Tulloch provide an interesting counterbalance to these approaches, inviting a more self-reflexive critical awareness and finding a balance between attention to the text and the meanings that audiences bring to texts by examining the functioning in culture of popular series/serial formats. Tulloch recognises that it is what people do with texts that ultimately matters while at the same time recognising that the structuring principles of TV drama and the ways in which these principles are employed by writers and producers may dispose some audiences towards some readings rather than others. Drawing on the work of Janet Woolf, the author in this context is understood as constituted discursively in language, ideology and social relations: 'the author being the first person to fix meanings which will of course subsequently be subject to redefinition and fixing by all future readers' (Woolf in Tulloch 1990: 17).

The application of the term 'generic' to a text implies that the text is a formulaic commercial product marked by recurring codes and conventions that are reproduced in text after text to meet audience demand for more of the same while satisfying expectations that it will not be exactly the same; some elements of the story will be a little bit different. Genre texts offer limited freedom within very definite limits – limits often prescribed by an agent on behalf of the broadcaster that is funding the production. They are reassuringly familiar, but with an interesting new twist or angle that makes them sufficiently exciting to entice the viewer. The 'difference' that individuates one genre text from others of its kind is kept within the limits of what commissioners deem acceptable, within reassuring structures of repetition and reiteration which ensure that audiences keep watching. If the production is successful with viewers and critics, much of the profit and acclaim rests with the company that commissioned it rather than the writer, a situation that La Plante refused to tolerate once she became aware of the commercial potential of her work.

The pattern of exclusion and dismissal of earlier female screenwriters and their work in the 1960s is beginning to become apparent in the critical evaluations of Lynda La Plante and her *oeuvre* since she has become an independent producer. As a creator of strong roles for women, she was initially judged a ground-breaking writer; awards were showered on her dramas and on their leading players Ann Mitchell (in 1983) and Helen Mirren (1991, 1992, 1993). When La Plante deviated from this pattern and turned to other themes, her works were generally considered less successful; thus *Civvies* was regarded by some critics as a 'dud' in spite of audiences in excess of eleven million and *Comics*, a more experimental, expressionistic piece, was regarded as 'sketchy' and 'unfinished'. La Plante, increasingly aware that the critical establishment was unsupportive of her work, attributed it to 'the peculiarly British phenomenon of "tall poppy syndrome", "build 'em up and knock 'em down"' (Rampton 1996). Surveying the press response to the dramas broadcast between 1996 and her writing award in 2001, she has good reason to feel rejected. Dramas written and produced for UK television in this period include *Supply and Demand* (ITV 1996), *Killer Net* (C4 1997), *Supply and Demand II* (ITV 1997), *Trial and Retribution II* (ITV 1998), *Trial and Retribution III* (ITV 1999), *Mind Games* (ITV 2000) and *Trial and Retribution IV* (ITV 2000). In their reviews of these dramas, critics often adopt a disdainful or mocking tone, condemning them for their violent content, clichéd scripts, predictable and/or exaggerated plotlines and weak characterisation. A brief analysis of the reception of La Plante's Internet murder mystery drama *Killer Net* (C4 1997) serves to illustrate the point.

The plot of *Killer Net* concerns two university students, Scott (Tam Williams) and Joe (Paul Bettany), who become hooked on the sexual thrills available from a US Internet site and sign up to receive a game called 'Killer Net' on compact disc advertised on the site. Playing the game involves committing a murder and disposing of the body without getting caught; players routinely have to complete a number of set tasks or activities before the next stage of the game is revealed. The game presumes that the players are male, the victims female, although Scott and Joe's flatmate Susie (Emily Woof), a nurse at a local hospital, also plays. Once the player has moved through various stages of play, successfully murdering and disposing of the body, he (*sic*) is rewarded by constructing a victim of his choice and playing the game again in order to kill her. Scott constructs an image of a woman he has met on-line and had a passionate affair with, Rich Bitch (Cathy Brolly). Rich Bitch, otherwise known as Charlotte, is the woman who introduces him to the world of Internet pornography and the murder game before dumping him. Several days after Scott has 'virtually' murdered Charlotte, her body is found dead in a copycat murder identical to the one in the game; Scott is arrested as the prime suspect. During the police investigation, the 'Killer Net' games master is revealed as an introverted computer programmer who murders the women constructed by the players, although in a further twist to the plot it transpires that he is not Charlotte's killer.

The detectives in *Killer Net* are literally paralysed in their attempts to understand the new media of computer games and the Internet. They do not possess the expertise, the technology or the imagination to investigate its possibilities for criminal activity. Scott tries to convince the police that he is innocent by inviting them to play the game; the police watch in horrified amusement as their caricatured simulacra appear on the screen. Their inability to understand the nature of the virtual world and its 'real life' parallels has serious consequences: a policewoman inserted into the game as a virtual decoy becomes the murderer's next victim and loses her life. The closing climax, with its chase sequence on Brighton pier, has resonances with the end of crime thrillers such as *Falling Down* (Schumaker 1993) and the female vigilante film *Dirty Weekend* (Winner 1993), only in this case the murderer kills his victim and escapes.

With its play on the erosion of difference between the 'real' of everyday life and the virtual reality of the game world, *Killer Net* touches on a number of contemporary concerns about the policing of boundaries. The drama pre-dates widespread concern about the use of the Internet for pornographic and paedophilic purposes, including the grooming of children and abduction of minors. In retrospect, its attempt to reveal the darker side of the Worldwide Web and its potential threat to young people seems prescient, but at the time La Plante was accused of finding yet another vehicle for pedalling her 'soft porn' fantasies. La Plante claims, as she does for all her dramas, that the ideas for *Killer Net* are rooted in actuality: she started playing computer games with her fifteen-year-old nephew and became aware that many of them contained extreme scenarios of violent rape and murder perpetrated by male characters. She hoped that the story would raise public awareness of the dangers of computer games and the Internet, in particular amongst parents with young children. In response to a critical account of the drama in the *Times*, she argues:

> *Killer Net* is a very moralistic piece and I hope the audience will learn about the devastation and destruction it can cause and just how deeply it can affect young people. My 15–year-old nephew asked me to play a computer game with him. I was shocked by the contents, which included rape and brutal deaths. There were scenes of such horror – far worse than the first *Alien* movie – which included a woman having her head bitten off. Yet it is the sort of game – games that encourage everything from the stealing of cars to the robbing of stores – that his age group are now buying without a thought. I want people to think hard about how urgently the Internet needs to be policed' (Hatley 1998: 10).

The vocal computer community were quick to leap to the defence of their occupation and point to the series' numerous technical errors and factual inaccuracies, including the use of obsolete jargon and terminology (Bennun 1998: 8). In the *Independent* Maxton Walker railed against the cultural stereotype of a computer expert depicted as an isolated nerd, unable to maintain interpersonal relationships: 'the bad guy turned out to be a weird, loner computer nerd. I'd urge people to flame Lynda La Plante' (Walker 1998:14).

Writ large in all these critiques was the question of realism: La Plante's principal offence, it seems, was to break the conventions of realism by creating implausible characters and situations. Critics dismissed *Killer Net* as 'a ridiculous middle aged fantasy', La Plante's on-line world as not only seedy but beyond credibility. She was accused of creating a new style of British non-realism, 'a pervasive and pointless modern idiom that probably has its roots in the success of *Shallow Grave* … Things are unreal, but never risk surrealism; there are spookily unexplained sources of light, unplaceable accents, fantastically humourless dialogue, very easy parking'. According to this critic, in British non-realism 'film-makers seek to do to Britain what Americans do to America: give extreme metaphorical resonance to place, attempt (vainly) to turn Brighton into "Brighton" … film fashions, writerly ignorance, and the requirements of the American market were all demanding untruth' (Lappin 1998: 53). The series' high production values – 'ravishingly good looking – all dark shadows and rich hues' – ultimately mirror the qualities of its subject: 'a triumph of style over substance'. The gist of these critiques is that La Plante has given stylish generic realism priority over authenticity of character and dialogue. The fact that Jason Orange, a former member of the boy band *Take That*, is cast for his star persona rather than his acting ability fuels this kind of criticism.

By abandoning realism in favour of a style of crime series designed for Channel 4, the most youth-orientated and 'America-friendly' of the UK terrestrial channels, La Plante unknowingly gave up a crucial factor in her authorial licence: her right as a dramatist to voice an opinion. She was accused of exploiting sexual content to tease viewers with glimpses of the seedy pleasures available on the Internet rather than approaching the subject with the 'proper seriousness' that traditionally signifies a non-exploitative treatment. Channel 4 was accused of broadcasting a 'gore-spattered shag-fest', of abdicating its public-service responsibilities – responsibilities that the Internet, as a carrier of private content, does not have. 'We are no more and no less at risk from the Internet than from the postal service or the phone network' pontificated the TV critic for the *Glasgow Herald*, intimating that TV influences us and our attitudes and behaviour but that the Internet has no such influence and because of this is absolved from any 'public' responsibility (Unattributed 1998: 15). In the *Daily Mail*, Peter Paterson continued his on-going critical assassination of La Plante's work that had begun with *Civvies* in 1992, while Joe Joseph in *The Times* managed to give her be-grudging credit for exploring the theme of on-line porn (Paterson 1998b; Joseph 1998). Female critics were no less condemnatory: Barbara Ellen in the *Observer* accused La Plante of having a 'smut fixation' and suffering delusions of visionary genius. In a telling final comment, she reveals the barometer she is using to judge La Plante: 'but Dennis Potter she ain't' (Ellen 1998: 66). In the tabloids and the broadsheets, local and national press, La Plante was called to account for replicating that which she was ostensibly condemning. As far as the critics were concerned, she had abandoned her mission of administering hard-hitting truths about the nature of our society in favour of pedalling cheap entertainment.

Quality and judgement

By the end of the 1990s, critical dislike of La Plante's work crystallises around four issues related to the concepts of authorship outlined above and the author's status as a writer of genre fiction: questions of aesthetic taste, her treatment of controversial contemporary issues, her pre-occupation with sexual violence and pornography and her commercial orientation. Taking each of these in turn and mapping them against the predominant trends in her work outlined earlier, a clear pattern of like and dislike emerges that has significant gender implications.

La Plante's most critically acclaimed work is undoubtedly *Prime Suspect*. As Deborah Jermyn argues, *Prime Suspect* was the most influential crime drama to emerge from Britain in the 1990s and has changed not only the British crime series, but the style of the crime genre internationally (Jermyn 2003). Although *Prime Suspect* was criticised, particularly by feminist critics, for its representations of women, the seriousness with which it treated its subject matter and the quality of the production values and acting in the series accorded with the critical tastes and evaluations of the television establishment, who, faced with the necessity of broadening their public-service remit, judged it an exemplary instance of the genre. By the middle of the decade, La Plante's work commanded prime-time slots on the two principal terrestrial channels, ITV and BBC 1. La Plante was in the unique position of being the most critically acclaimed and the most popular television dramatist in Britain, a position never held by any other writer. During this time she also produced hard-hitting dramas (*Civvies, Seconds Out* and *Comics*) with violent content that examined male working lives and aspects of the social construction of masculinity. Critics located these in the tradition of 'commitment' drama, realism and the single play. Although not always well received, these dramas were respected for their 'messages', for their attempts to grapple with contentious issues within a framework of public-service values that was shifting to accommodate the expanding multi-channel environment.

Once La Plante left *Prime Suspect* and took control of her own productions, critical opinion began to shift. In part this is because her work becomes more melodramatic; she gives free rein to her delight in spectacle and starts to create dramas that are distinctly more playful, such as *She's Out* and *Bella Mafia*. The pleasures on offer in these dramas are distinctly different to those of her more experimental and socially engaged work and arguably more 'feminine' in their audience address. It is interesting to note in this context that *Bella Mafia* was treated far more dispassionately by US television critics than UK commentators; they took note of the excellent performances and delighted in its commitment to melodramatic excess, all values derided by British critics, who continue to disparage melodrama as a 'low-brow' form. Within this context of shifting critical opinion, *Killer Net* is not one of La Plante's most synthesised works; stylistically, it falls awkwardly between the realist claims of 'commitment' drama, the generic realism of the crime series and melodramatic stylisation, an uneasy alliance that leaves her open to accusations of the gratuitous use of violence.

For similar reasons, La Plante has received little praise for the more experimental aspects of her work. *Killer Net* deserves credit for its entertaining attempt to depict new forms of interactivity between the narrative formats of different media – television drama, computer games and the Internet – now accepted as commonplace. Behind the scenes at ITV drama in the late 1990s, there was considerable interest in harnessing the creative and marketing potential of emergent and converging technologies to develop the first interactive television drama. Sponsored by the ITV network, in 1998 the on-line ITV Drama Forum actively solicited ideas for various forms of reality TV and interactive drama.[10] Julian Favre, in an overview of developments in interactive fiction, points to the difficulties of adapting drama for interactive platforms, primarily because of the expense and the technical difficulties. Most programming relies on what Favre terms 'enhanced narrative'; viewers cannot interact with the story, but they can interact with a dedicated TV application broadcast at the same time as the drama that offers access to additional content and interactive features related to the show. These include additional information about the characters, summaries of episodes to date, trivia, surveys and opportunities to purchase related goods (Favre 2002). World Production's *Attachments* (BBC 2 2000) had an accompanying website of this type; although the drama was successful, its innovative aspects received little by way of critical attention. Producers are particularly interested in developing multi-path narratives that allow viewers to change the endings of stories, but these are expensive to produce because alternative paths of the story have to be made. Other variations include the ability to follow one character within a story or one strand of a story, a possibility introduced by La Plante in the split-screen format of *Trial and Retribution*.

As a female independent producer who has successfully 'penetrated' the male-dominated business of television drama production, La Plante can give free expression to her creative and business inclinations. She is an astute businesswoman who knows that if she wants continuing success at home, she has to play to the market and her existing fan base. Within this context, it is unsurprising that dramas commissioned for the ITV network such as *The Commander* (ITV 2002), starring former *Silent Witness* lead Amanda Burton, and *Trial and Retribution 7* (2003) reiterate successful 'blockbuster' formulae repackaged for viewers who enjoy La Plante's psychological thrillers and feisty female characters. Not content with her UK fan base, La Plante also seeks success on a global scale, trading her products on the international market. By the end of the 1990s, US television drama faced increasing international competition from producers such as Teleglobo (Brazil) whose spectacular telenovellas had found a wide and appreciative audience in countries as different as Mexico, Russia and the former communist states of Eastern Europe (Buonanno 2000). With melodrama and generic realism rather than British social realism the mode of drama that travels interculturally and sells well in the global marketplace, La Plante's work has increasingly adopted these characteristics.

During the course of a long career La Plante has changed her persona from actor to successful writer to successful businesswoman. Like many successful writers of popular fiction, she keeps a firm grasp on the market and is accustomed to exercising her personal judgement. She has always worked most successfully within popular generic frames, never claiming that she is writing about the human condition, only that what she writes is based on thorough research and that her dramas attempt to be accurate about the kinds of worlds depicted, the characters portrayed. If during the course of her work she has touched on prescient themes and rattled us out of our complacency as viewers, it is because she strives to entertain while always being mindful of the broader social tensions that inform her stories. Undoubtedly, *Prime Suspect* will stand as an enduring legacy of her contribution to the British crime thriller, not least because, as Jermyn (2003) notes, it has influenced the crime thriller internationally. As La Plante moves into the world of feature-film production, it will be interesting to see if the film medium is more suited to her contemporary idiom than the small-screen world of television drama or whether her lasting legacy will be the creation of the character who first brought her critical and popular international acclaim, DCI Jane Tennison.

Notes

1 *Timecode* divides the screen into four sections, each of which focuses on a character's interlinked story. 24 uses the split screen to change the focus of attention and remind viewers of contingent and parallel time frames and action as the drama unfolds in 'real' time.

2 Channel 5 was the last terrestrial channel to go on air in the UK, in 1997; see Fanthome 2003.

3 *Widows* was finally produced in 2000 as a four-hour mini-series for ABC starring Mercedes Ruehl, Brooke Shields and Rosie Perez. La Plante was executive producer.

4 La Plante resisted pressure from TV executives to make DCI Jane Tennison younger on the basis of character authenticity. Kate Buffery of *Trial and Retribution* has been less fortunate; La Plante replaced her at the end of series five with a younger leading female.

5 Action vehicles such as westerns and chase films were referred to as melodramas by the Hollywood industry. The use of the term 'melodrama' to describe emotional

dramas centred on female protagonists was developed by feminist critics in the 1970s; see Neale 2000.

6 *A Man Called Ironside* (Harbour/Universal) was broadcast on BBC 1 from 1967 to 1976. In the US, the show was known as *Ironside*. Raymond Burr played the veteran wheelchair-bound former detective and lawyer Robert Ironside.

7 *The Godfather* (1972), *The Godfather Part II* (1974), *The Godfather Part III* (1990). Coppola's daughter Sofia plays the daughter of Godfather Michael Corleone (Al Pacino) in the third film.

8 Award-winning percussionist Evelyn Glennie and co-composer Greg Malcangi were nominated for a BAFTA award for the *Trial and Retribution* soundtrack.

9 Robin Nelson argues that the cutting rate and the rapid turnover of narrative segments in all TV drama increased exponentially in the 1990s in tandem with aestheticisation of the image. 'Flexi-narratve' is the term he uses to denote the fast-cut multi-narrative structures, 'flexiad' a visual style that echoes advertisements and pop videos in the deployment of signifiers for their intrinsic 'values and lifestyle' appeal rather than used in their referential sense to denote the 'real'. See Nelson 1997: 24–5.

10 ITV-Drama Forum.com, visited regularly during 1998; the site is no longer active.

Appendix
Works by Lynda La Plante

Works for UK television

Widows Thames TV/Euston Films 1983

6 × 1-hour episodes; weekly serial (winner of BAFTA best direction)
Executive Producer: Verity Lambert
Producer: Linda Agran
Director: Ian Toynton

Widows II Thames TV/Euston Films 1985 (sequel)

6 × 1-hour episodes; weekly serial
Executive Producers: Linda Agran, Johnny Goodman
Producer: Irving Teitelbaum
Director: Paul Annett

Prime Suspect Granada 1991

2 × 2-hour mini-series
Executive Producer: Sally Head
Producer: Don Leaver
Director: Christopher Menaul

Civvies BBC Wales 1992

6 × 1-hour episodes; weekly serial
Producer: Ruth Caleb, Ruth Kenley-Letts
Director: Karl Francis

Framed Anglia Films/Tessauro Arts and Entertainment Network 1992

2 × 2-hour mini-series

Executive Producer: Delia Fine, Brenda Reid
Producer: Guy Slater
Associate Producer: Laura Julien
Director: Geoffrey Sax

Prime Suspect II Granada 1992 (written with Alan Cubbitt)

2 × 2-hour mini-series
Executive Producer: Sally Head
Producer: Paul Marcus
Director: John Strickland

Seconds Out Screen One, Granada Television/BBC 1 1992

90-minute film
Producer: Simon Passmore
Associate Producer: Mathew Hamilton
Director: Bruce MacDonald

Comics Cinema Verity/C4 1993

2 × 2-hour mini-series
Producers: Verity Lambert, Selwyn Roberts
Director: Dairmuid Lawrence

Prime Suspect III Granada 1993

2 × 2-hour mini-series
Executive Producer: Sally Head
Producer: Paul Marcus
Associate Producer: Lynda La Plante
Director: David Drury

Seekers A Lawson Production/Central TV 1993

2 × 2-hour mini-series
Producer: Sarah Lawson
Director: Peter Barber-Fleming

The Lifeboat Bloom Street Productions/BBC Wales 1994

9 × 50-minute episodes; weekly series
Storyline and first two episodes by Lynda La Plante
Executive Producers: Ruth Caleb, Karl Francis, Lynda La Plante

Producer: Ruth Kenley-Letts
Directors: Karl Francis, Dewi Humphreys, Emlyn Williams

She's Out Cinema Verity and La Plante Productions/Carlton TV 1995

6 × 1-hour episodes; weekly serial
Producer: Verity Lambert
Associate Producer: Lynda La Plante
Director: Ian Toynton

The Governor A La Plante Production for the ITV network 1995

2 hour pilot film and 5 × 1-hour episodes; weekly series
Executive Producer: Steve Lanning
Producer: Lynda La Plante
Directors: Alan Dosser, Rob Knights, Bob Mahoney

The Governor II A La Plante Production for the ITV network 1996

6 x 1-hour episodes; weekly series
Producer: Lynda La Plante
Directors: Aisling Walsh, Rob Knights, Bob Mahoney

Supply and Demand A La Plante Production for the ITV Network 1996

2-hour television film
Writers: Lynda La Plante and Steve Griffiths
Executive Producer: Steve Lanning, Keith Richardson
Producer: Lynda La Plante
Associate Producer: Liz Thorburn
Director: Peter MacDonald

Trial and Retribution A La Plante Production for the ITV network 1996

2 × 2-hour mini-series
Executive Producer: Steve Lanning, Keith Richardson
Producer: Lynda La Plante
Associate Producer: Liz Thorburn
Director: Aisling Walsh

Killer Net A La Plante Production for C4 1997

4 × 1-hour episodes; weekly serial
Executive Producer: Steve Lanning

Producer: Lynda La Plante
Director: Geoffrey Sax

Supply and Demand II A La Plante Production for the ITV network
1997

6 × 1-hour episodes; weekly series
Producer: Lynda La Plante
Associate Producer: Liz Thorburn
Director: Waris Hussein, Colin Bucksey

Trial and Retribution II A La Plante Production for the ITV network 1998

2 × 2-hour mini-series
Executive Producer: Keith Richardson
Producer: Lynda La Plante
Associate Producer: Liz Thorburn
Director: Aisling Walsh

Trial and Retribution III A La Plante Production for the ITV network
1999

2 × 2-hour mini-series
Producers: Lynda La Plante, Peter Richardson
Associate Producer: Liz Thorburn
Director: Jo Johnson

Mind Games A La Plante Production for the ITV network 2000

Producers: Lynda La Plante, Peter Richardson
Associate Producer: Liz Thorburn
Director: Richard Standeven

Trial and Retribution IV A La Plante Production for the ITV network
2000

2 × 2-hour mini-series
Executive Producer: Peter Richardson
Producer: Lynda La Plante
Associate Producer: Liz Thorburn
Director: Michael Whyte

Trial and Retribution V A La Plante Production for the ITV network 2001

2 × 2-hour mini-series
Producer: Lynda La Plante
Associate Producer: Liz Thorburn
Director: Aisling Walsh

The Commander A La Plante Production for the ITV network 2002

Producer: Lynda La Plante
Director: Michael Whyte

Trial and Retribution VI A La Plante Production for the ITV network 2002

2 × 2-hour mini-series
Producer: Lynda La Plante
Director: Ferdinand Fairfax

Trial and Retribution VII A La Plante Production for the ITV network, 2003

2 × 2-hour mini-series
Producers: Lynda La Plante and Peter McAeese
Director: Charles Beeson

Works for US television

The Prosecutors A La Plante Production and Scripps Howard Entertainment production for NBC 1997

2-hour television film
Written by Lynda La Plante and Tom Fontana
Producers: Tom Fontana, Lynda La Plante, Julie Martin
Co-producer: Billy Higgins
Director: Rod Holcomb

Bella Mafia CBS 1997

4-hour mini-series
Executive Producer: Lynda La Plante
Producer: Frank Konigsberg
Director: David Greene

Cold Shoulder New Regency/CBS 2000

1-hour pilot
Executive Producer: Lynda La Plante
Producer: Jeff Morton
Director: Charles Haid

The Warden TNT 2000

Adaptation of *The Governor* written by Natalie Chaidaz
2-hour pilot
Executive Producers: Lynda La Plante, Jon Cowan, Robert Rovner
Producers: David Roessell, Natalie Chaidez
Director: Stephen Gyllenhaal

Widows ABC 2000

4-hour mini-series
Executive Producer: Lynda La Plante
Producer: Clara George
Director: Geoff Sax

Framed TNT 2001

Adapted from Lynda La Plante's *Framed* (1992) by Daniel Petrie Jr
Executive Producer: Lynda La Plante
Director: Daniel Petrie Jr

Novels

The Legacy (1987) London, Sidgwick & Jackson
The Talisman (1989) London and New York, Pan
Bella Mafia (1991) London and New York, HarperCollins
Entwined (1992) London, Sidgwick & Jackson
Cold Shoulder (1994) London and New York, Pan Macmillan
Cold Blood (1996) London and New York, Macmillan
Cold Heart (1998) London and New York, Macmillan/Random House
Sleeping Cruelty (2000) London and New York, Macmillan
Royal Flush (2002) London and New York, Macmillan
Royal Heist (2004) New York, Random House
Above Suspicion (2004) New York, Simon & Schuster

Novels of television series

Widows (1983) London, Sphere Books
Widows II (1985) London, Mandarin
Prime Suspect I (1991) London and New York, Pan
Prime Suspect II (1992) London, Mandarin
Prime Suspect III (1993) London, Mandarin
Civvies (1992) London, Mandarin
Framed (1992) London, Mandarin
Seekers (1993) London and New York, Pan/HarperCollins
The Lifeboat (1994) London, Mandarin
She's Out (1995) London and New York, Pan Macmillan
The Governor (1995) London and New York, Pan Macmillan
The Governor II (1995) London and New York, Pan Macmillan
Trial and Retribution (1997) London and New York, Pan Macmillan
Trial and Retribution II (1998) London and New York, Pan Macmillan
Trial and Retribution III (1999) London and New York, Pan Macmillan
Trial and Retribution IV (2000) London and New York, Pan Macmillan
Trial and Retribution V (2002) London and New York, Pan Macmillan
Trial and Retribution VI (2002) London and New York, Pan Macmillan

Bibliography

Alderson, K. (1995) 'I've never felt the need to become one of the boys', *The Times*, 16 June.

Allen, C. (1998) 'Netting a prime suspect', *The Times*, 1 May; Features.

Alley, R. and R. Brown (2001) *Women Television Producers: Transformation of the Male Medium*, Rochester, NY, University of Rochester Press.

Alsop, N. (1984/5) 'Leather to Lacey', *Primetime*, 9: 16-19.

Alvarado, M. and J. Stewart (eds) (1985) *Made for Television: Euston Films Limited*, London, British Film Institute.

Andermahr, S. (1994) 'A queer love affair? Madonna and lesbian and gay culture' in D. Hamer and B. Budge (eds), *The Good, the Bad and the Gorgeous: Popular Culture's Romance with Lesbianism*, London and San Francisco, Pandora: 28-40.

Ansorge, P. (1997) *From Liverpool to Los Angeles: On Writing for Theatre, Film and Television*, London, Faber and Faber.

Association of Cinematograph and Television Technicians (1975) *Patterns of Discrimination Against Women in the Film and Television Industries*, London, ACTT.

Auty, M. (1985), 'But is it cinema?' in M. Auty and N. Roddick (eds) *British Cinema Now*, London, British Film Institute.

Baehr, H. (1980a) 'The "liberated woman" in television drama', *Women's Studies International Quarterly*, 3: 29–39.

Baehr, H. (ed.) (1980b) *Women and Media*, Oxford, New York, Toronto, Pergamon Press.

Baehr, H. (1981) 'Women's employment in British television', *Media, Culture and Society*, 3 (2): 125–34.

Baehr, H. and G. Dyer (eds) (1987) *Boxed In: Women and Television*. New York and London, Pandora.

BBC (1992) *Extending Choice in the Digital Age*, www.digitaltv.culture.gov.uk

Beck, A. (ed.) (2003) *Cultural Work: Understanding the Cultural Industries*, London, Routledge.

Bedell, G. (1993) 'Where bigotry is part of the job; a policewoman tells of victory over racial and sexual abuse', *Independent*, 12 December: 8.

Benedict, D. (1994) 'I love all that cut, cut, cut', *Independent*, 2 December: 25.

Bennet, T., S. Boyd-Bowman, C. Mercer and J. Woollacott (eds) (1981) *Popular Television and Film*, London and Milton Keynes, BFI Publishing/ Open University Press.

Bennun, D. (1998) 'Net losses, few gains', *Guardian*, 18 May: 8.

Benton, S. (1975) 'Patterns of discrimination against women in the film and television industries', *Film and Television Technician*, March.

Berkeley, D. (2003) 'Creativity and economic transactions in television drama production' in A. Beck (ed.) *Cultural Work: Understanding the Cultural Industries*, London, Routledge: 103–20.

Bignell, J. and S. Lacey (eds) (2005) *Popular Television Drama*, Manchester, Manchester University Press.

Bignell, J., S. Lacey and M. Macmurraugh-Kavanagh (eds) (2000) 'Editors' introduction' in *British Television Drama: Past, Present and Future*, Basingstoke and New York, Palgrave: 1–23.

Billen, A. (1996) 'The Andrew Billen interview', *Observer Life Magazine*, 3 March: 6.

Billingham, P. (2000) *Seeing the City through Television*, Exeter, Intellect.

Bird, L. and Fliot, J. (1993) '*The Life and Loves of a She-Devil*' (Fay Weldon– Ted Whitehead) in George W. Brandt (ed.) *British Television Drama in the 1980s*, Cambridge, Cambridge University Press: 214–33.

Brandt, G. (ed.) (1981) *British Television Drama*, Cambridge, Cambridge University Press.

Brandt, G. (ed.) (1993) *British Television Drama in the 1980s*, Cambridge, Cambridge University Press.

Brenton, H. (2003) *Front Row* BBC Radio 4, 10 June.

Brown, M. E. (ed.) (1990) *Television and Women's Culture: The Politics of the Popular*, London, New Delhi, Thousand Oaks, Sage.

Brunsdon, C. (ed.) (1986) *Films For Women*, London, BFI Publishing.

Brunsdon, C. (1987) 'Men's genres for women' in H. Baehr and G. Dyer (eds) *Boxed In: Women and Television*, New York and London, Pandora: 184–202.

Brunsdon, C. (1990) 'Problems with quality', *Screen* 31 (1): 67–90.

Brunsdon, C. (1997) 'Post-feminism and shopping films' in *Screen Tastes: Soap Opera to Satellite Dishes*, London and New York, Routledge: 81–102.

Brunsdon, C. (1998) 'Structure of anxiety: recent British TV crime fiction', *Screen* 39 (3): 223–43.

Brunsdon, C. (2000) 'Not having it all: women and film in the 1990s' in R. Murphy (ed.) *British Cinema of the 1990s*, London, BFI.

Brunsdon, C., J. D'Acci and L. Spiegel (eds) (1997) *Feminist Television Criticism: A Reader*, Oxford, Oxford University Press.

Budge, B. (1988) 'Joan Collins and the wilder side of women' in L. Gammon and M. Marshment (eds) *The Female Gaze: Women as Viewers of Popular Culture*, London, The Women's Press.

Buonanno, M. (ed) (1999) *Shifting Landscapes: Television Fiction in Europe*, Luton, University of Luton Press.

Buonanno, M. (ed.) (2000) *Continuity and Change: Television Fiction in Europe*, Luton, University of Luton Press.

Buscombe, E. (1976) 'The Sweeney – better than nothing', *Screen Education* 20: 66–9.

Buscombe, E. (2000) *Television Studies: A Reader*, Oxford, Oxford University Press.

Buxton, D. (1990) *From the Avengers to Miami Vice: Form and Ideology in Television Series*, Manchester, Manchester University Press.

Campbell, B. (1985) 'Outlaws with class', *City Limits*, 5 April: 13–15.

Campbell, D. (1995) 'One more murder on her mind: DCI Jeanette Joyce has no time for distractions', *Scotland on Sunday*, 19 January.

Carson, B. (2000) 'Cultural hybridity, masculinity and nostalgia in the TV adaptation of *The Buddha of Surburbia*' in B. Carson and M. Llewellyn-Jones (eds) *Frames and Fictions: The Politics of Identity within Drama*, Exeter and Oregon, Intellect: 113–25.

Cartmell, D., I. Q. Hunter, H. Kaye and I. Whelehan (eds) *Sisterhoods*, London and Sterling, VA, Pluto Press.

Caughie, J. (1991) 'The logics of convergence' in J. Hill and M. McCloone (eds) *Big Picture, Small Screen: The Relations between Film and Television*, Luton, John Libby/University of Luton Press.

Caughie, J. (2000a) *British Television Drama: Realism, Modernism and British Culture*, Oxford, Oxford University Press.

Caughie, J. (2000b) 'What do actors do when they act?' in J. Bignell, S. Lacey and M. Macmurraugh-Kavanagh (eds) *British Television Drama: Past, Present and Future*, Basingstoke and New York, Palgrave: 162–74.

Clarke, J. (1995) 'Super Sandra', *Daily Record*, 25 March: 4.

Collins, M. (1992) 'The mind as a combat zone', *Guardian*, 4 November: 10.

Cook, J. (ed.) (1982) *Television Sitcom*, BFI Dossier 17, London, British Film Institute.

Cook, J. (1995) *Dennis Potter: A Life on Screen*, Manchester, Manchester University Press.

Copjec, J. (ed.) (1993) *Shades of Noir: A Reader*, London, Verso.

Corner, J. (1996) *The Art of Record*, Manchester, Manchester University Press.

Coward, R. (1978) 'Sexual liberation and the family', *M/F*, 1: 7–23.

Coward, R. (1987) 'Dennis Potter and the question of the television author', *Critical Quarterly* 29 (4): 79–88.

Craig, P. and M. Cadogan (1981) *The Lady Investigates: Women Detectives and Spies in Fiction*, Oxford and New York, Oxford University Press.

Creeber, G. (1998) *Dennis Potter: Between Two Worlds, A Critical Reassessment*, London and New York, Macmillan.

Creeber, G. (2001a) 'Cigarettes and alcohol: investigating gender, genre and gratification in *Prime Suspect*', *Television and New Media* 2 (2): 149–66.

Creeber, G. (2001b) 'The mini-series' in G. Creeber (ed.) *The Television Genre Book*, London, British Film Institute: 35–8.

Creeber, G. (2001c) 'Intimacy, continuity and memory in the TV drama serial', *Media, Culture and Society* 23: 439–55.

Crisell, A. (1997) *An Introductory History of British Broadcasting*, London, Routledge.

Curran, J. and J. Seaton (2003) *Power without Responsibility: The Press and Broadcasting and New Media in Britain*, London, Routledge.

D'Acci, J. (1994) *Defining Women: Television and the Case of Cagney and Lacey*, Chapel Hill, NC, University of North Carolina Press.

Davies, C. (1996) 'The sociology of professions and the profession of gender', *Sociology* 30 (4): 661–78.

Davies, K., J. Dickey and T. Stratford (eds) (1987) *Out of Focus: Writings on Women and the Media*, London, The Women's Press.

Day-Lewis, S. (1998) *Talk of Drama*, Luton, University of Luton Press.

Diawara, M. (1993) 'Noir by Noirs: toward a new realism in black cinema' in J. Copjec (ed.) *Shades of Noir: A Reader*, London, Verso: 261–77.

Diski, J. (1993) 'Skeletons and corpses', *Sight and Sound* 3 (1): 4.

Duncan, A. (2003) 'The sleuth is still out there', *Radio Times*, 8 November: 18–21.

Dyer, R. (1979, 1998) *Stars*, London, BFI.

Dyer, R., C. Geraghty, M. Jordan, T. Lovell, R. Paterson and J. Stewart (1981) *Coronation Street*, London, BFI.

Eaton, M. (1995) 'A fair cop? canteen culture in *Prime Suspect* and *Between the Lines*' in D. Kidd-Hewitt and R. Osborne (eds) *Crime and the Media: The Postmodern Spectacle*, London, Pluto Press: 164–84.

Edgar, D. (2000) 'Playing shops, shopping plays: the effect of the internal market on television drama' in J. Bignell, S. Lacey and M. Macmurraugh-Kavanagh, *British Television Drama: Past, Present and Future*, London and New York, Palgrave: 73–7.

Edgecombe, M. (1985) 'Thanks a million ...', *News of the World, Sunday Magazine*, 31 March: 16, 18.

Ellen, B. (1998) 'Television: Tuesday 5 May' *Observer*, 3 May: 66.

Elley, D. (1993), '*Prime Suspect 3*', *Variety* 430 (9): 57.

Evans, G. (1992) 'La Plante passed over by Hollywood', *Evening Standard*, 18 June: 10.

Faludi, S. (1992) *Backlash: The Undeclared War Against Women*, London, Vintage.

Fanthome, C. (2003) *Channel 5: The Early Years*, Luton, University of Luton Press.

Favre, J. (2002) 'Formats in interactive fiction parts 1–7', Interactive Television International, *http://iemmys.tv/itvi/archive/feature*, accessed 24 August 2003.

Feuer, J. (1995) *Seeing Through the Eighties: Television and Reaganism*, Durham, NC and London, Duke University Press.

Feuer, J., P. Kerr and T. Vahimagi (1985) *MTM: 'Quality Television'*, London, BFI Publishing.

Finch, J., M. Cox and M. Giles (eds) (2003) *Granada Television: The First Generation*, Manchester, Manchester University Press.

Fiske, J. (1987) *Television Culture*, London, Methuen.

Francis, P. (1997) 'Why the loss of a child is close to my heart', *TV Times*, October 18: 18-20.

Francis, S. (1995) *Today*, 7 May: 20.

Frank, A. (1994) 'Under-covered agent', *The Times*, Features, 19 March.

Gallagher, M. (1980) *Unequal Opportunities: The Case of Women and the Media*, Paris, Unesco.

Gallagher, M. (1984) *Employment and Positive Action for Women in the Television Organisations of the EEC Members States*, Brussels, Commission of the European Communities.

Gallagher, M. (1985) *Unequal Opportunities: Update*, Paris, Unesco.

Gammon, L. and M. Marshment (eds) (1988) *The Female Gaze: Women as Viewers of Popular Culture*, London, The Women's Press.

Garfield, S. (1990) 'That's why the lady is a vamp', *Independent*, 25 November: 27.

Gilbert, W. Stephen (1997) *Fight, Kick and Bite: The Life and Work of Dennis Potter*, London, Hodder and Stroughton.

Giles, M. (2003) 'A square peg' in J. Finch, M. Cox and M. Giles (eds) *Granada Television: The First Generation*, Manchester, Manchester University Press: 38–42.

Giles, P. and V. Lorish (eds) (1992) *Debut on Two*, London, BBC Books.

Gilligan, C. (1993) *In a Different Voice*, Harvard, Harvard University Press.

Gledhill, C. (ed.) *Stardom: Industry of Desire*, London, Routledge: 167–82.

Glover, G. (1996) 'Fiery engine', *Scotsman*, 17 June: 15.

Goodwin, P. (1998) *Television Under the Tories: Broadcasting Policy 1979–1997*, London, BFI Publishing.

Grant, S. (1992) 'Plante plots', *Time Out* , 23 September: 23.

Gripsrud, J. (1995) *The Dynasty Years: Hollywood Television and Critical Media Studies*, London and New York, Routledge.

Gritten, D. (1993) 'La plume de La Plante', *Daily Telegraph Magazine*, 29 May: 38, 40–1.

Hall, S. (1988) *The Hard Road to Renewal: Thatcherism and the Crisis of the Left*, London, Verso.

Hall, S., C. Critcher, T. Jefferson, J. Clarke and B. Roberts (1978) *Policing the Crisis: Mugging, the State, Law and Order*, London, Macmillan.

Hallam, J. (1998) 'Gender and professionalism in the medical melodrama' in N. Moody and J. Hallam (eds) *Medical Fictions*, Liverpool, Association for Popular Fiction/Liverpool John Moores University Press: 25-45.

Hallam, J. (2000a) *Nursing the Image: Media, Culture and Professional Identity*, London, Routledge.

Hallam, J. (2000b) 'Gender, genre and Lynda La Plante' in J. Bignell, S. Lacey and M. Macmurraugh-Kavanagh (eds) *British Television Drama: Past, Present and Future*, London and New York, Palgrave: 140–9.

Hallam, J. (2005) 'Remembering *Butterflies*: the comic art of housework' in J. Bignell and S. Lacey (eds) *Popular Television Drama*, Manchester, Manchester University Press.

Hallam, J. and M. Marshment (1995) 'Framing experience: case studies in the reception of *Oranges Are Not the Only Fruit'*, *Screen* 36 (1): 1–15.

Hallam, J. with M. Marshment (2000) *Realism and Popular Cinema*, Manchester, Manchester University Press.

Haralovich, M. B. (1999) *'I Spy's* "living postcards": the geo-politics of Civil Rights' in M. B. Haralovich and L. Rabinovitz (eds) *Television History and American Culture: Feminist Critical Essays*, Durham, NC and London, Duke University Press: 98–119.

Hatley, R. (1998) 'TV dredges the depths of the net', *The Times* Inter/Face, 15 April: 10–11.

Hayward, A. and A. Rennert (1996) *Prime Suspect: The Official Book of the Award-Winning Series*, London, KQED Books, Carlton Books/Granada Television.

Hildred, S. (1995) *'She's Out'*, ITV', *Sun*, 11 April: 15.

Hill, J. (1986) *Sex, Class and Realism*, London, BFI Publishing.

Hill, J. and M. McLoone (eds) (1996) *Big Picture, Small Screen: The Relations Between Film and Television*, Luton, John Libbey/University of Luton Press.

Hobson, D. (1982) *Crossroads: The Drama of a Soap Opera*, London, Methuen.

Hollows, J. (2000) *Feminism, Femininity and Popular Culture*, Manchester, Manchester University Press.

Honeyford, S. (1980) 'Women and television' *Screen* 21 (2): 49–52.

Hulse, T. (1997) 'The writer who was lost for words', *Sunday Telegraph Magazine*, 26 October: 18, 20–1.

Hunt, L. (1999) 'Dog eat dog: *The Squeeze* and the *Sweeney* films' in S. Chibnall and R. Murphy (eds) *British Crime Cinema*, London, Routledge: 134–47.

Hurd, G. (1981) 'The television presentation of the police' in T. Bennet , S. Boyd-Bowman, C. Mercer and J. Woollacott (eds) *Popular Television and Film*, London and Milton Keynes, BFI Publishing/Open University Press: 53–70.

Huyssen, A. (1986) 'Mass culture as woman: modernism's other' in *After the Great Divide: Modernism, Mass Culture, Postmodernism*, Bloomington, IN, Indiana University Press: 44–62.

Hyem, J. (1987) 'Entering the arena: writing for television' in H. Baehr and G. Dyer (eds) *Boxed In: Women and Television*, New York and London, Pandora: 151–63.

Iley, C. (1992) 'Iron fist in a Velvet Glove', *Sunday Times*, 27 September: Features.

Jansson, S. (1998) 'The difference of viewing: female detectives in fiction and in film' in D. Cartmell, I. Q. Hunter, H. Kaye and I. Whelehan (eds) *Sisterhoods*, London and Sterling, VA, Pluto Press: 149–66.

Jefferies, S. (1992) 'Nightmare on civvy street', *Guardian*, 23 September.

Jennings, R. (1998) 'The "prime" of DCI Tennison: investigating notions of feminism, sexuality, gender and genre in relation to Lynda La Plante's *Prime Suspect'*, *Iris*, 26: 177–89.

Jermyn, D. (2003) 'Women with a mission: Lynda La Plante, DCI Tennison and the reconfiguration of TV crime drama', *International Journal of Cultural Studies*, 6 (1): 46–63.

Jones, M. (1994) 'My greatest influence', *Daily Mail Weekend*, 24 October: 7.

Joseph, J. (1998) 'Out in the desert, beyond reach of parody', *The Times*, 6 May: Features.

Kaplan, A. ([1978] 1998) *Women in Film Noir*, London, BFI Publishing.

Kidd-Hewitt, D. and R. Osborne (eds) (1995) *Crime and the Media: The Postmodern Spectacle*, London, Pluto Press.

Kilfoyle, P. (2000) *Left Behind: Lessons from Labour's Heartland*, London, Politico's.

King, B. (1991) 'Articulating stardom' in C. Gledhill (ed.) *Stardom: Industry of Desire*, London, Routledge: 167–82.

King, J. and M. Stott (eds) (1977) *Is This Your Life? Images of Women in the Media*, London, Virago/Quartet Books.

Koerber, C. (1977) 'Television' in J. King and M. Stott (eds) *Is This Your Life? Images of Women in the Media*, London, Virago/Quartet Books: 123–42.

Krutnik, F. (1991) *In a Lonely Street: Film Noir, Genre, Masculinity*, London, Routledge.

Kuhn, A. (1982), *Women's Pictures: Feminism and Cinema*, London, Routledge and Kegan Paul.

La Plante, L. (1992) 'All policemen must face up to charges of bias', *Sunday Telegraph*, 26 July: 4.

La Plante, L. (1998) 'I was so excited, typing away' in S. Day-Lewis (ed.) *Talk of Drama*, Luton, University of Luton Press.

Lacey, S. (2005) 'Becoming popular: some reflections on the relationship between television and theatre' in J. Bignell and S. Lacey (eds) *Popular Television Drama*, Manchester, Manchester University Press.

Lappin, T. (1998) 'Chic thrill', *Scotland on Sunday*, Sunday Spectrum, 31 May: 53.

Lawson, M. (1998) 'Queen of the inside track', *Guardian*, 17 October: 86–7.

Lawson, M. (2000) 'Drama queen', *Guardian*, 2 October: 17.

Lee, J. (1988) 'Care to join me in an upwardly mobile tango? Postmodernism and the New Women' in L. Gammon and M. Marshment (eds) *The Female Gaze: Women as Viewers of Popular Culture*, London, The Women's Press: 166–73.

Macdonald, M. (1995) *Representing Women: Myths of Femininity in the Popular Media*, London, New York, Sydney, Edward Arnold.

Macmurraugh-Kavanagh, M. K. (1999) 'Boys on top: gender and authorship on the BBC Wednesday Play 1964–70', *Media, Culture and Society* 21 (3): 409–25.

Macmurraugh-Kavanagh, M. K. (2000a) 'Too secret for words: coded dissent in female-authored *Wednesday Plays*' in J. Bignell, S. Lacey, M. Macmurraugh-Kavanagh (eds) *British Television Drama: Past, Present and Future*, Basingstoke and New York, Palgrave: 150–62.

Macmurraugh-Kavanagh, M. K. (2000b) 'What's all this then? The ideology of identity in *The Cops*' in B. Carson and M. Llewellyn-Jones, *Frames and Fictions: The Politics of Identity within Drama*, Exeter and Oregon, Intellect: 40–9.

Malik, S. (2002) *Representing Black Britain: Black and Asian Images on Television*, London, Thousand Oaks, New Delhi, Sage.

Manuel, Preethi (1987) 'Black women in British television drama – a case of marginal representation' in K. Davies, J. Dickey and T. Stratford (eds) *Out of Focus: Writings on Women and the Media*, London, The Women's Press.

Marshall, P. David (1997) *Celebrity and Power: Fame in Contemporary Culture*, Minneapolis and London, University of Minnesota Press.

Medhurst, A. and L. Tuck (1982) 'The gender game' in J. Cook (ed.) *Television Sitcom*, BFI Dossier 17, London, British Film Institute: 43-55.

Miller, R. (1996) *Mystery, A Celebration: Stalking Public Television's Greatest Sleuths*, San Francisco, KQED Books.

Mirren, H. (1994) Interview: 'Oh to be over there and overpaid; here she's highly acclaimed; in Hollywood she's a nobody. How can they snub Helen Mirren?' *Independent*, 22 March: 21.

Modleski, T. (1982) *Loving with a Vengeance*, Methuen, New York.

Moir, J. (1992) 'The Jean Moir interview', *Guardian*, 6 May: 19.

Monroe, J. (1998) 'ROM for your life', *Time Out*, 29 April: 16.

Morgan, E. (1979) 'Writing for television: women's contribution' in *Women's Studies International Quarterly*, 2: 209-13.

Morley, D. (1986) *Family Television: Cultural Power and Domestic Leisure*, London, Comedia.

Munt, S. (1994) *Murder by the Book*, London, Routledge.

Neale, S. (2000) *Genre and Hollywood*, London, Routledge.

Neale, S. and F. Krutnik (eds) (1990) *Popular Film and Television Comedy*, London, Routledge.

Nelson, R. (1997) *TV Drama in Transition*, London, Macmillan.

Nelson, R. (2001) 'Studying televison drama' in G. Creeber (ed.) *The Televison Genre Book*, London, BFI Publishing: 8–11.

Nightingale, B. (1994) 'Theatre', *The Times*, 16 April.

Paterson, P. (1992a) 'No medals for misfit paras', *Daily Mail*, 23 September: 36.

Paterson, P. (1992b) 'La Plante's feeble fighting farce', *Daily Mail*, 5 October: 30.

Paterson, P. (1998a) 'A vile trial for us all', *Daily Mail*, 20 October: 55.

Paterson, P. (1998b) 'Caught in an evil net', *Daily Mail*, 6 May: 55.

Paterson R. (1999) 'Accommodating to the market or creating quality?' in M. Buonanno (ed.) *Shifting Landscapes: Television Fiction in Europe*, Luton, University of Luton Press.

Pearson, A. (1995) *Observer Review*, 16 October: 1.

Philips, D. (2000) 'Medicated soap: the woman doctor in television medical drama' in B. Carson and M. Llewellyn-Jones (eds) *Frames and Fictions: The Politics of Identity within Drama*, Exeter and Oregon, Intellect: 113–25.

Pines, J. (1995) 'Black cops and black villains in film and TV crime fiction' in D. Kidd-Hewitt and R. Osborne (eds) *Crime and the Media: The Postmodern Spectacle*, London, Pluto Press: 67–77.

Place, J. A. (1978) 'Women in film noir' in A. Kaplan, *Women in Film Noir*, London, BFI Publishing: 35–67.

Place, J. A. and L. S. Peterson ([1974] 1996) 'Some visual motifs of film noir' in A. Silver and J. Ursini (eds) *Film Noir Reader*, New York, Limelight: 65-76.

Plater, A. (2000) 'The age of innocence' in J. Bignell, S. Lacey, M. Macmurraugh-Kavanagh (eds) *British Television Drama: Past, Present and Future*, Basingstoke and New York, Palgrave: 68–72.

Potter, D. (1993) 'Occupying powers', *Guardian Outlook*, 28 August: 21.

Powell, R. (1992) 'RTS drama award pacifies La Plante', *Broadcast*, 5 June: 12.

Power, V. (1997) 'Is TV getting away with murder?', *TV Times*, 18 October: 20–1.

Purser, P. (1991) Interview with Lynda La Plante, *Daily Telegraph*, 10 April.

Rampton, J. (1996) 'Prime-time with Lynda La Plante', *Independent*, 22 March.

Rennert, A. (ed) (1995) *Helen Mirren: A Celebration*, San Francisco, KQED Books.

Rolfe, G. (1993) 'A fair cop', *Daily Mail*, 18 December: 38.

Ross Muir, A. (1988) 'The status of women working in film and television' in L. Gamman and M. Marshment (eds) *The Female Gaze*, London, The Women's Press: 143–52.

Royal Television Society (1993) 'Prime writing', *Television* 30 (4): 10–11.

Schatz, T. (1988) *The Genius of the System: Hollywood Filmmaking in the Studio Era*, New York, Pantheon Books.

Scott, T. (1992) '*Prime Suspect I–III*', *Variety*', 20 January: 144.

Silver, A. and J. Ursini (eds) (1996) *Film Noir Reader*, New York, Limelight.

Simms, M. (1985) *Women in BBC Management*, London, BBC.

Simpson, P. (ed.) (2002) *The Rough Guide to Cult TV*, Harmondsworth, Penguin.

Skeggs, B. (1997) *Formations of Class and Gender: Becoming Respectable*, London, New Delhi, Thousand Oaks, Sage.

Skirrow, G. (1985) '*Widows*' in M. Alvarado and J. Stewart (eds) *Made for Television: Euston Films Limited*, London, British Film Institute: 174–84.

Skirrow, G. (1987a) 'Representation of women in the Association of Cinematograph, Television and Allied Technicians', *Screen*, 22 (3): 94–102.

Skirrow, G. (1987b) 'Women, acting, power' in H. Baehr and G. Dyer (eds) *Boxed In: Women and Television*, New York and London, Pandora: 164–83.

Smith, A. (1998) *Television: An International History*, 2nd edn, Oxford, Oxford University Press.

Smith, J. ([1989] 1992) *Misogynies*, London, Faber and Faber.

Sparks, R. (1992) *Television and the Drama of Crime: Moral Tales and the Place of Crime in Public Life*, Buckingham and Philadelphia, Open University Press.

Spigel, L. and D. Mann (eds) (1992) *Private Screenings: Television and the Female Consumer*, Minneapolis, University of Minnesota Press.

Staff reporter (1995) *Evening Standard*, 16 May: 15.

Stoddart, P. (1985) *Broadcast*, 19 April: 78.

Stoddart, P. (1992) 'Woman with a macho pen', *Daily Telegraph*, 19 September: 6.

Summers, S. (1992) 'I hope to God this *does* cause a stir', *Independent*, 23 September: 15.

Sutton, S. (1982) *The Largest Theatre in the World: Thirty Years of Television Drama*, London, BBC.

Sweeting, A. (1998) 'More like a weed than a Plante', *Guardian*, 25 June.

Tasker, Y. (1998) *Working Girls: Gender and Sexuality in Popular Cinema*, London, Routledge.

Thornham, S. (1994) 'Feminist interventions: *Prime Suspect 1*', *Critical Survey* 6 (2): 226–33.

Thornham, S. (2003) 'A good body: the case of/for feminist media studies', *European Journal of Cultural Studies* 6 (1): 75–94.

Thumim, J. (ed.) (2002) *Small Screens, Big Ideas: Television in the 1950s*, London, IB Taurus.

Tuchman, G., A. K. Daniels and J. Benet (eds) (1978) *Hearth and Home: Images of Women and the Media*, Oxford, Oxford University Press.

Tulloch, J. (1990) *Television Drama: Agency, Audience and Myth*, London and New York, Routledge.

Tulloch, J. and M. Alvarado (1983) *Doctor Who: The Unfolding Text*, London, Macmillan.

Turner, G. (1994) 'When success forces you to compromise your sexuality', *Daily Mail*, 6 July: 50.

Tylee, C. (2000) 'The black explorer: female identity in black feminist drama on British television in 1992' in B. Carson and M. Llewellyn-Jones (ed.) *Frames and Fictions: The Politics of Identity within Drama*, Exeter and Oregon, Intellect: 100–12.

Unattributed (1995) 'Meet the real Governor behind new TV drama', *Evening Standard*, 16 May: 15.

Unattributed (1998) 'It came as a shock really', *Glasgow Herald*, 9 May: 15.

Walker, M. (1998) 'Is this for real?', *Independent*, 30 May: 14.

Walton, P. and M. Jones (1999) *Detective Agency: Women Re-writing the Hard-Boiled Tradition*, Berkeley, Los Angeles, London, University of California Press.

Weale, S. (2000) 'Tale with a twist', *Guardian*, Section 2, 4 October: 16.

White, L. (1995) 'Prime crime', *Sunday Times Magazine*, 26 February: 38, 41–2, 44.

Willis, J. and S. Dex (2003) 'Mothers returning to television production work in a changing environment' in A. Beck (ed.) *Cultural Work: Understanding the Cultural Industries*, London and New York, Routledge.

Women's Broadcasting Committee and BECTU (1993) *Her Point of View*, London, Women's Broadcasting Committee and BECTU.

Wueratna, A. (1996) 'Hometown: Lynda La Plante: Crosby', *The Times Magazine*, 28 December: 42.

Index